FAMILY TREASURY OF ART

GIOTTO
VAN EYCK
PIERO
BOTTICELLI
BOSCH
LEONARDO
DURER
MICHELANGELO
RAPHAEL
TITIAN
HOLBEIN
BRUEGEL
EL GRECO
RUBENS
HALS
VELAZQUEZ
REMBRANDT
VERMEER
GAINSBOROUGH
TURNER
Family
GOYA
DELACROIX
DAUMIER
MANET
DEGAS
CEZANNE
MONET
RODIN
RENOIR
ROUSSEAU
RYDER
EAKINS
GAUGUIN
VAN GOGH
SEURAT
TOULOUSE-LAUTREC
KANDINSKY
MATISSE
ROUAULT
MONDRIAN
KLEE
LEGER
PICASSO
BRAQUE
MODIGLIANI
CHAGALL
MIRO
MOORE
DE KOONING
POLLOCK

Samm Sinclair Baker and Natalie Baker

Treasury of Art

Galahad Books • New York City

Dedicated with love to all the
wonderful young people in "Bakey's"
art classes over the past years...
who have learned, as we have, that
"the secret of life is in art."

All rights reserved. No part of this work may be reproduced or transmitted in any form or by any means, electronic or mechanical, including photocopying, recording, or any information storage and retrieval system, without permission in writing from the publisher.

First published in the United States of America in 1981 by
GALAHAD BOOKS
95 Madison Avenue
New York, New York 10016
By arrangement with Harry N. Abrams, Inc., New York
This book originally appeared under the title *Introduction to Art*

Library of Congress Catalog Card Number: 81-81164
ISBN: 0-88365-567-5

Printed in Japan

Contents

AUTHORS' NOTE

This book opens a door for you into the wonderful world of art . . .

Follow us through that door and let us introduce you to many of the greatest artists, show you how they lived and worked, what they thought and felt. You will learn some of the secrets of how and why great art is created by men of genius. You will learn, too, that the world of art is rich and many-sided, a place where you can always find something to appeal to your special interest, your particular mood.

The enjoyment of art follows an understanding of art. The aim of this book is to lead you through understanding to that enjoyment which can only be an enriching and broadening experience, because at all times and places talented men and women have given us their dreams, their vision of beauty and perfection, their response to good and evil, life and death, the great truths of existence.

They have shown us that the lowly and humble can be noble, that the charm of fleeting moments can be valuable forever, and that, though our world has boundaries, the human imagination has no limits. The artist, by means of his extraordinary talent, can make us see things we never dreamed existed, and can show us the familiar in such a different aspect that we are obliged to alter our own viewpoint, if not to broaden it.

No form of art is "better" than any other; each simply speaks to us in a different way. In this book we have put many kinds of art before you, with the hope that you will agree that there are no absolute rules of what is good or bad in art.

A feeling for art awakens the senses and enables us to be more keenly aware of the beauties of nature, on the one hand; and on the other, more responsive to creative artists, ancient and modern, who in their various ways have commented on human experience. May you be inspired to seek out and learn more, always more, about art. Thus you will increase your enjoyment by having a heightened response to all beauty through the rest of your life.

FAMILY TREASURY OF ART

Giotto *About 1266–1337*

Supposed Self-Portrait. 1305–6. *This detail from the fresco series in the Arena Chapel is believed to be a self-portrait. It was not unusual for an artist to include himself in his paintings among a crowd of spectators.*

GIOTTO, A GREAT PIONEER OF PAINTING, created a new art form in his time. He broke away from the medieval tradition of painting flat, stiff, unreal figures, and instead created forms of a bulk and roundness almost like sculpture—more alive and full of emotion. His powerful work influenced artists in his day and Italian art for centuries thereafter.

He was honored as a master, yet his genius sprang from the humblest conditions. There is a story that Giotto, about ten years old, was tending his father's sheep. To pass the time, he scratched animals on flat stones. One day the noted artist Cimabue saw Giotto drawing, immediately became excited about such a young talent, and persuaded the child's father to let him work in his studio, the busiest in Florence. There the boy helped clean brushes and grind colors while learning to draw and paint.

Giotto progressed swiftly. He painted religious scenes with such sympathy and beauty that the stories and people seemed to come alive. He grew into a fine, learned man, and his work was in great demand. The poet Dante wrote:

Cimabue thought to hold the field
As painter, but everybody praises Giotto's name
So that he obscures the fame of the other.

In his thirties, Giotto went to Rome and studied classical styles of sculpture and painting. Most Italian artists of the thirteenth century painted on wooden panels, but Roman artists still used the technique of ancient times which became known as *fresco* painting—painting with colors on wet plaster which had been freshly applied to a wall. Perhaps it was here in Rome that Giotto learned about fresco painting, which he used later in his "picture cycles" (the illustration of a continuing story in a series of panels). He decorated part of the Church of San Francesco in Assisi, and made thirty-seven frescoes in the Arena Chapel in Padua.

As his art beautified a number of Italian cities, Giotto gained increasing fame as an artist and architect. In his workshop in Florence, he taught many students. He began a magnificent bell tower in Florence, to be built next to the Cathedral. He died before it was finished and was buried in the Cathedral. His tomb is marked by a plain marble slab, not unlike the flat stones on which he scratched drawings as a youthful shepherd.

Flight into Egypt. 1305–6. *This is one of the frescoes in the Arena Chapel, which were the most original paintings of the early fourteenth century in Italy. Everything, including color, is simplified, partly to center interest on the main subject. The people at the bottom of the picture seem like actors on a stage, brought so close to us that we feel we are moving along with them. The solid forms of the figures are revealed through their clothing. Note how the lines of the rock clefts appear again in the folds of the robes, uniting background and figures. The angel seems to fly right at us—such a realistic effect had never before been achieved in painting.*

Saint Francis Gives His Cloak to a Poor Knight. About 1296–1300. *Giotto is said to have painted the legend of Saint Francis, helper of the poor, in a series of twenty-eight frescoes in the Upper Church of San Francesco in Assisi. Giotto pictured people acting naturally, looking at each other, as in the tender gestures of giving and taking the robe in this scene. This is an unusually detailed but solid landscape, which adds to the dramatic moment of the gift. The V-shape of the hills fixes our eyes right on the head of the saint. The triangular and curving patterns—the line of the horse's bowed neck repeats the curve of the poor man's back—give the picture a lovely rhythm.*

The Lamentation over Christ. About 1305–6. *Many consider this Giotto's masterpiece, filled with a pathos new to art at that time. The massive and expressive figures, dramatic gestures (particularly the outstretched arms of the central figure), and mournful faces create an intense feeling of deepest sorrow. The tortured angel adds to the effect of grief and loss, as may be seen in the detail at right.*

Jan van Eyck *About 1390–1441*

JAN VAN EYCK, the most famous Flemish artist of the fifteenth century, must be credited with some of the greatest advances in art, notably in his use of oil paints, his rendering of space and light, and his close observation of nature. Jan was a deeply religious man as well as a supremely gifted artist. In all his works he pictured reality in the tiniest details, and so poetically that each masterpiece seems to be in praise of a God who made all this wonderful nature.

Nothing is known of Jan's early years, but documents show that he worked in Holland in 1422–24. Then, in 1425, he was appointed Court Painter to Philip the Good, Duke of Burgundy, a post he held until 1429. Jan also acted as a diplomat for the duke, who sent him to Spain and Portugal. He spent the remainder of his life in Bruges, an artistic center in Flanders. Of his older brother Hubert little is known, except that he worked on the great *Ghent Altarpiece*, and that he died in 1426.

The Van Eyck brothers, though perhaps not the inventors of oil painting, were certainly among the first to use it successfully. Medieval painters had used tempera, a type of paint in which colors were mixed with water and egg yolks. Colors mixed with oil produced a very slow-drying medium that was so fluid that the artist could create many new subtle effects of light, color, and detail. Jan could apply many thin and filmy, or thick and non-transparent layers of paint to the surface of the wooden panel. These alternating layers, in varying shades of light and dark colors, produced soft-edged forms enveloped in a hazy light.

It was this magical light that created a sense of depth, by making some objects seem clear and thus close to us, and others seem to dissolve, as if far away in the distant landscape. This revolutionary process began a whole new era of art—painters found that they could create a much wider range of shades of colors, and record the most intricate details and patterns. Oil became the basic medium of painting for the next five hundred years.

Man in a Red Turban. 1433. *With Jan van Eyck's superb paintings of individuals, portraits were in demand more than ever, especially in the court of the Duke of Burgundy. At that time artists were beginning to paint sitters' heads in the three-quarter view. Although no one knows just what Van Eyck looked like, some experts note that this man's eyes squint, as if he was looking into a mirror while painting—so this may be a self-portrait. Van Eyck has made it an exquisite picture through his use of a brilliant red in the large, elaborately wrapped turban.*

◀ OPPOSITE PAGE

Giovanni Arnolfini and His Bride. 1434. *It is thrilling to study the hundreds of tiny items in this masterpiece. At first glance we see an Italian merchant and his bride in their home, taking their marriage vows. Looking further, we see the reflection in the mirror of two more figures standing before the couple; one of them may be the artist, who printed on the wall:* Johannes de eyck fuit hic *(Jan van Eyck was here). Note a separate little painting in each of the ten circles on the mirror frame. You see almost every silky hair on the dog; every tiny facet of the chandelier; the grain of the floorboards and wooden shoes; the carving of the bedstead; and much more. Many of these objects have a symbolic meaning for marriage, such as the dog for fidelity. By careful distribution of layers of light and dark colors, Van Eyck brought all these elements together into a unified whole—all in a work less than three feet by two feet in size.*

Jan van Eyck CONTINUED

Virgin Mary, *from the* Ghent Altarpiece. About 1424–32. *According to the inscription on the frame, this altarpiece was begun by Hubert, and finished by Jan in 1432. It is the greatest masterpiece of the northern European school of artists known as the Early Netherlandish School. It is made up of over twenty panels. Here is one panel, a sample of the vast scope of the work. Van Eyck was a master at picturing all kinds of surfaces, whether cloth, stone, or skin. In the detail (at left), every pearl glows, each gem gleams, every hair shines. Van Eyck also included in the crown types of lilies and roses, flowers which represent the purity of the Virgin.*

Saint Barbara. 1437. *With a sensitive hand, Van Eyck here portrayed a saint of such delicacy that we feel that the slightest breeze, but for her voluminous robe, would lift her to heaven. The drawing is alive with workmen all around and even atop the unfinished tower. Look for the men on horseback at left, four women to the right of the saint, countless trees in the far-stretching landscape, and even a flight of geese in the sky. All these details blend in uncrowded harmony in a drawing only about eleven inches high.*

Piero della Francesca *About 1415–1492*

King Solomon Receiving the Queen of Sheba. 1452–59. *This scene from the same series of frescoes shows the queen telling Solomon about her vision. In order to make the scene dramatic, Piero used fresh colors and pale light rather than excited gestures. Note again how he has created the sense of space between the carefully placed figures so that we can feel the distance between the figures standing in front of and behind the king. The fresco has been damaged at the right, and the blue of the king's underrobe has disappeared. To make blue colors for frescoes, artists used ground blue gems (they used earth pigments to make other colors), which, for chemical reasons, usually disappeared or turned green.*

The Resurrection. About 1463. *In one of Piero's greatest religious paintings, Christ emerges from the tomb while the soldiers sleep. This fresco was hidden by whitewash for a hundred years before it was rediscovered. It is thought that the artist may have painted himself as the sleeping soldier second from left. Note the carefully balanced, geometric composition of the Renaissance period: the men's heads and Christ's knees form a triangular shape within a larger triangle made by the outlines of the whole figures, and the triangle is balanced at the top by a row of trees. The banner and the soldier's lance lead our eyes to trees, which in turn lead us into the deep landscape.*

MANY EXPERTS CONSIDER PIERO the greatest artist of the Early Renaissance in Italy. Known in his day as "the monarch of painting," his fame has grown through the centuries. He is recognized as a supreme master of color and composition, and is unsurpassed in creating the quality of light. Standing before his masterpieces, one feels a magic, ethereal beauty; a critic once said that Piero's work "sings in pure lyric tones."

Born in Borgo San Sepolcro, a village in the Italian province of Tuscany, he later returned frequently to his beloved home. As a youth he studied in Florence with the painter Domenico Veneziano, who was seeking fresh, almost pastel-like colors to reflect soft, clear light. Piero continued this search in all his years of painting.

The ability to show the roundness of natural forms, and to show people in action, had been developed before Piero's time in the masterful work of Giotto, and that of Masaccio, who died in 1428. Perspective—the placement of objects in space and the creation of an illusion of depth in painting—had gained importance in the art of Paolo Uccello, a few years older than Piero. Thus Piero could profit from the discoveries of these artists: he learned to make solid figures and objects, and to blend them in harmony with their background. He did this by creating an atmosphere of clear light that flowed around, into, and out of his figures, and by arranging his forms in a composition that was mathematically perfect in all its proportions and perspective. Yet Piero's work has been called "cold," possibly because his approach was intellectual rather than emotional. Today his paintings are regarded with great respect, if not awe, for their purity of design and clarity of form.

A mathematician as well as a painter, Piero in his later years wrote essays on perspective and mathematics. He wrote: "Painting consists of three parts: drawing, perspective, coloring." He never married, and spent the last part of his life in Borgo San Sepolcro. He did not do any painting after about 1478, for he became blind. A man of great sensitivity, his ideal was a blend of art, science, and religion, which he tried to convey in his works. Their special quality has defied imitation, and has remained unmatched through the centuries.

The Queen of Sheba. 1452–59. *This is a portion of one of the frescoes in the Church of San Francesco in Arezzo in Tuscany. It is part of a series,* The Legend of the True Cross, *in which the artist depicted the history of the cross on which Christ was crucified. In this scene the Queen of Sheba has a vision while traveling to see King Solomon. As she kneels in prayer at a bridge, a portion of which will be used to make the cross, there is a feeling that time has stopped. The quiet sadness of the scene is deeply moving. Here we can see how the crystal-clear light, which reminds us of white moonlight, seems to surround the figures.*

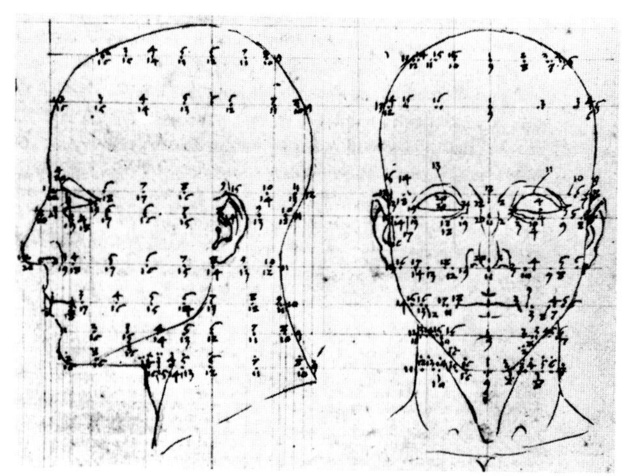

Geometric Head Designs—Front and Profile. About 1480. *In his essays on drawing and perspective, Piero the mathematician showed humans and objects in great detail. He contributed much to the science of perspective, and to the understanding of form, space, depth, and light.*

The Victory of Heraclius over Chosroes. 1452–59. *In this great battle painting from* The Legend of the True Cross, *Piero crowded many warriors together, using a wide variety of postures, gestures, shapes, and colors. Yet he avoided confusion by combining the elements in a continuous row running across the picture, adding relief in the airy, floating banners. The kneeling figure at right—the defeated Chosroes, King of Persia—is about to be beheaded.*

The Duke and Duchess of Urbino. 1465. *With powerful simplicity, Piero painted these solemn faces high above the horizon of the vast landscape. He portrayed the sitters without flattery, but with affection, as they were both his friends and patrons. See how he recorded every detail, including the duke's wrinkles and moles, and his famous nose. On the back of this diptych (a painting of two panels), Piero painted imaginative figures symbolizing the virtue and greatness of the duke and duchess.*

Botticelli *About 1444–1510*

SANDRO BOTTICELLI (Filipepi Alessandro; called Botticelli or "little barrel") is the great *poetic* artist of the Italian Renaissance. Turning his back on political and religious unrest during his younger years, Botticelli created a personal vision of beauty. He changed the natural forms of trees and flowers, as well as people, to suit his imaginative vision. His masterpieces are filled with graceful, melancholy figures moving as in slow motion.

It became clear early that the boy was poor at schoolwork but a genius at drawing. He studied in Florence with a noted artist, Fra Filippo Lippi, who influenced the youngster's delicate approach to art. Botticelli grew up to be a gentleman—sensitive, faithful to friends, and deeply religious.

In creating symbolic, decorative pictures, he chose pagan gods and goddesses as romantic subjects for colorful story-telling. The rich, ornamental beauty of his work made him a favorite artist of the court of the Medici, the family which ruled Florence. There he mingled with the foremost artists, scholars, and poets of the age, and was respected by them. As his fame spread, he received many commissions for paintings, including works for Pope Sixtus IV in the Sistine Chapel in Rome.

Botticelli's very individual, charming style can easily be recognized by his curving, graceful figures and his delicate lines. He used muted colors to help hold together the many elements in his pictures. As his style matured, his colors became more brilliant, though he still cared little about light-and-dark modeling. His work remained gentle, romantically sad, and unrealistic. He died a lonely man, having done little or no painting in his last ten years. It was not until over 350 years after his death that the world recognized his importance in art.

Primavera (Allegory of Spring). About 1478. *This is one of Botticelli's most prized decorative works. It is a poet's dream—even the flowers, leaves, and fruit are a stylization of nature's beauty. The gentle spirit of Spring shimmers over the canvas. A chubby cupid aims his arrow at the Three Graces at left, who form one of the most lyrically painted groups in all art, their filmy robes swirling rhythmically with the turning of their bodies. In the center Venus faintly gestures her blessing, while Flora, in a flowered gown, scatters petals. Winged and robed in blue, Zephyrus, the wind, blows upon a nymph of the Hours from whose mouth issue forth flowers. The lovingly painted curves and arches lead our eyes through the exquisite picture, as if we were watching a ballet.*

Self-Portrait. About 1476. *This detail from his masterwork,* The Adoration of the Magi, *is believed to be the face of the artist, one of over thirty persons pictured. He stares at us as if he were looking into a mirror while painting his self-portrait. Botticelli has portrayed himself as a handsome, dreamy poet. He painted many such elegant portraits, lacking flesh-and-blood warmth, because he always sought to create ideal beauty in a graceful, harmonious design.*

Drawing for Dante's Divine Comedy *(detail).* About 1490–97. *Botticelli was one of the most brilliant draftsmen of the Renaissance, but most of his drawings have disappeared. Between 1490 and 1497 he made a series of drawings to illustrate a copy of* The Divine Comedy *belonging to a Florentine nobleman. Fortunately, many of these drawings have been preserved. In this example, Botticelli's fine, flowing lines of the praying or weeping figures re-create the intense, spiritual mood of this epic poem about heaven and hell.*

The Annunciation. 1490. *Botticelli painted several pictures of the Annunciation (the angel Gabriel telling Mary that she was to give birth to Jesus). His later works, mostly religious paintings, are much deeper in feeling than the artist's early, more decorative pictures. There is a tragic air in the gestures and expressions of Gabriel and the Virgin, as though they know of the Crucifixion to come.*

Madonna of the Magnificat. About 1485. *Based on the Magnificat, a hymn to the Virgin Mary, this is the most famous of Botticelli's* tondi *(round paintings). Marvelously designed to fit the circle, the scene reveals Botticelli's deeply religious feeling and sense of idealized beauty. The lovely Madonna, the sensitive coloring, and the flowing lines all combine in glorious harmony, as in sacred song. His divine women are a clearly recognizable "Botticelli type"—charming, soft, and gentle.*

Bosch About 1450–1516

The Garden of Earthly Delights. About 1500. *Many of Bosch's works were triptychs (paintings divided into three panels). This triptych, his largest masterpiece, is crowded with human figures, monsters, and strange creatures representing both good and evil. The secret meanings of the hundreds of weird but enchanting images have long puzzled and fascinated scholars. No one is sure today what the details really mean. The panel at left shows the Garden of Eden—a strange, beautiful view of paradise on earth. The center panel shows men and women supposedly engaging in sinful activities in an imaginative landscape of huge plants and flowers. The panel at right is the dark hell of man's own making, in which eerie musical instruments have become machines of torture manned by demons. Note how Bosch used many clear, bright, and cheerful colors and pleasing forms in the scenes of the garden at left and center, while at right he used dark, violent colors and grotesque shapes to create the horrors of hell.*

Hieronymus Bosch was a crusader against evil, using paintbrushes as his weapons. He seems not to have borrowed ideas from other artists, but to have created his wondrous fantasies with his own highly original mind. His nightmare creatures and visions, both strange and complicated, challenge our imaginations today.

This artist of unusual genius spent his life in the medieval, walled-in town of s'Hertogenbosch, in what is now Holland. The town was rather isolated from the Renaissance movement—it is interesting to note that Bosch worked at the same time as such artists as Raphael

CONTINUED ON PAGE 27

Supposed Copy of a Self-Portrait. About 1550. *This drawing of a grim, stringy-necked old man with lively, piercing eyes is thought to be a copy made after a late self-portrait of Bosch. Through delicately drawn details attention is fixed on the head, while only sparse lines are used for the figure.*

Altarpiece of the Temptation of Saint Anthony. About 1500. *Bosch liked to paint stories of saints who became hermits. In this triptych, in each of three scenes he surrounded Saint Anthony with temptations and devils which he would conquer with his faith. Evil creatures haunt the earth and sky. In the distance, a city is being destroyed by fire (a theme used often in Bosch's work). Here the artist has successfully combined the many figures, objects, and structures into a unified, rhythmic pattern. And by using a deep landscape setting, he was able to add many small details.*

Details of Altarpiece of the Temptation of Saint Anthony. About 1500. *Here are three details from the altarpiece that show typical demons of Bosch's imagination. In the detail at right, strange creatures bear a praying Saint Anthony through the air. They are combinations of toads, fishes, and some unidentifiable animals. The above detail shows "The Devil's Messenger" as an odd creature on ice skates, with the lower part of his beak a handy spike for carrying notes. The left detail is an example of the way in which Bosch pictured heretics and disbelievers—part man, part beast, and part imaginary forms.*

Bosch CONTINUED

and Leonardo in Italy. An honored local artist, Bosch also belonged to the Brotherhood of Our Lady, an association which influenced his life and his art. The Brotherhood held prayer meetings and funeral services, helped the poor, and encouraged music, theater, and religious ornamentation. Bosch made designs for some stained-glass windows, and several altarpieces for the town church, but nothing remains today. He became known all over Europe for his fantasizing pictures, but there are no records to show whether he traveled to other countries.

Experts have argued for centuries about the meaning of Bosch's fantasies. There is general agreement that the devout artist was preaching to sinners through his pictures: he tried to show how people were straying from true Christian beliefs, falling into sin and madness, and thus helping the devil's army to destroy mankind. Many people of his time were God-fearing, superstitious, afraid of the Devil and of their own possible fate. Bosch no doubt meant his paintings to frighten people into forsaking sinfulness for more righteous conduct, by showing how evil demons torment wicked humans with pain and illness.

Technically, Bosch painted with a light, free touch, and his numerous details delight rather than frighten us today. His work reveals a masterly sense of color and draftsmanship. His paintings, though the products of his very personal dream world, at the same time give us a dramatic portrayal of the Late Middle Ages.

Leonardo da Vinci *1452–1519*

Self-Portrait. About 1512. *In his last few years Leonardo lived in a small castle in France given to him by King Francis I, who visited him every day. At that time he may have made this superb drawing in red chalk, showing himself as an old, old man (though at the time he was really about sixty). Leonardo is one of the finest draftsmen in the history of art. He made thousands of drawings covering a wide range of subjects, but this is his only known likeness.*

THREE ARTISTS—Leonardo, Michelangelo, and Raphael—were the leaders of the Italian Renaissance. Leonardo, the oldest of the three, was the most inventive, many-sided genius of the period: scientist, mathematician, inventor, engineer, architect, musician, writer, sculptor, and painter. (To this day, a man who uses his abilities well in many areas may be called "a Renaissance man.")

By 1469 Leonardo had gone to live in Florence with his father, and had entered the workshop of the painter and sculptor Verrocchio. It is said that the handsome youth had an amazingly keen mind and showed his genius in everything he tried. Yet throughout his life Leonardo would start things and not finish them, because he would continually become interested in different projects. Never satisfied, he tried to learn about everything; he wrote: "The natural desire of good men is knowledge."

In his early portraits and religious paintings Leonardo developed a soft, poetic style, while retaining his scientific interest in depicting all the details of nature. As his fame spread he received important commissions, such as the large painting, *Adoration of the Magi*, which he never completed. About 1482 the Florentine ruler Lorenzo de' Medici, who is also known as Lorenzo the Magnificent, sent Leonardo as a musician to present a silver lyre to Ludovico Sforza, Duke of Milan. Leonardo is said to have played the lyre wonderfully well. He stayed at the court of Milan for seventeen years, painting, inventing machines, and planning buildings, bridges, dams, and monuments.

For two years Leonardo worked slowly and painstakingly on his huge masterpiece, *The Last Supper*. On one day he would arrive very early, climb a high scaffolding, and work until nightfall without eating or drinking. On another day he would just sit, study the picture, perhaps

CONTINUED ON PAGE 30

OPPOSITE PAGE ▶

Mona Lisa. About 1503. *This may be the world's best-known painting. Leonardo did not use the popular profile portrait, but painted an elegant woman gazing at you with a strangely calm yet haunting look. The mysterious quality of the portrait is achieved by Leonardo's special application of light and shadow, called* sfumato *(smoke), which softens the outlines of forms instead of creating hard edges. This creates a mistiness in the air which melts the landscape into the distance, yet at the same time enfolds the head and figure, thus unifying the whole scene.* Sfumato *was one of Leonardo's noted artistic devices, and was taken over by many of his followers.*

The subtle smile of the Mona Lisa *seems to glow from within. Cover her mouth, and her eyes still reflect mystery and suggest a smile.*

Leonardo da Vinci CONTINUED

dab at a figure or two, and then leave. The result was one of the most famous and important works in the history of art, but it has not lasted well. Leonardo experimented unsuccessfully with the technique of fresco painting, and the paint soon peeled from the wall. It was practically in ruins by the mid-sixteenth century.

Leonardo also visited Venice, returned to Florence, where he worked as Architect and Engineer-in-Chief to Cesare Borgia, the notorious warlord of the Renaissance, and spent his last years in France. Leonardo still found time to paint and to study nature, and when he died at sixty-seven he left thick notebooks crammed with sketches and teachings on art, philosophy, anatomy, plants, warfare, and numerous other subjects.

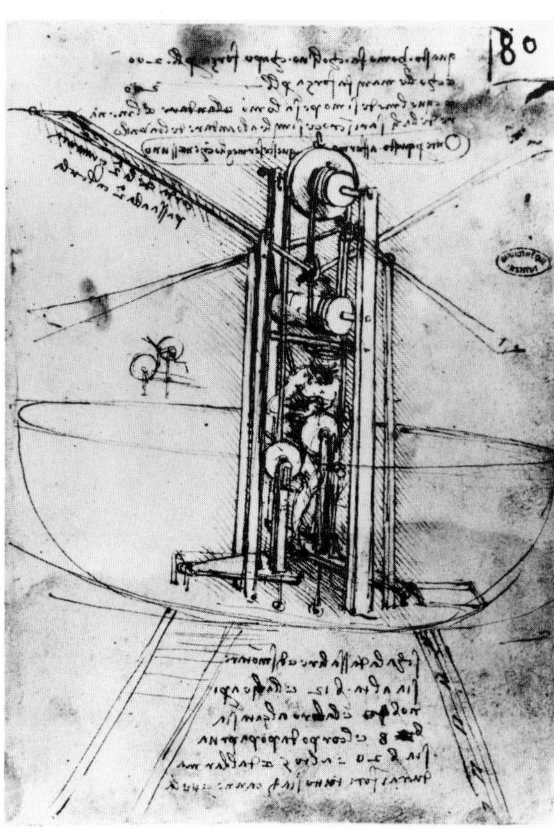

Flying Machine. About 1495. *Leonardo's inventive genius produced diagrams for flying machines, war machines, guns, tanks, and many other devices, centuries before they became reality. In this drawing he shows exactly what the operator of the machine should do: he must work the pulleys to make the wings move up and down. Leonardo's notes about his inventions, which we see here above and below the sketch, were written* backwards—*it is said that he wrote backwards partly to keep his ideas a secret.*

Baptism of Christ *(detail)*. About 1470–72. *It is believed that the angel at left was painted by the young Leonardo, and the one at right by his teacher, Verrocchio. Note how much more sensitively and gracefully modeled Leonardo's angel is. Already we see his fascination with drapery folds and the shadows they create. Throughout his life he made drapery studies, working out the fall of cloth over parts of the body.*

OPPOSITE PAGE ▶

Virgin of the Rocks. Unfinished, begun about 1483. *This deeply religious, poetic masterwork shows clearly how Leonardo tried to unite ideal beauty with carefully observed naturalism. The plants and rocks are exquisitely formed to the last detail, though they seem to melt away in the deep shadows. Note how the tender gestures of the hands, and the loving expressions of the faces, bathed in warm light, enhance the already perfect unity of the pyramidal composition.*

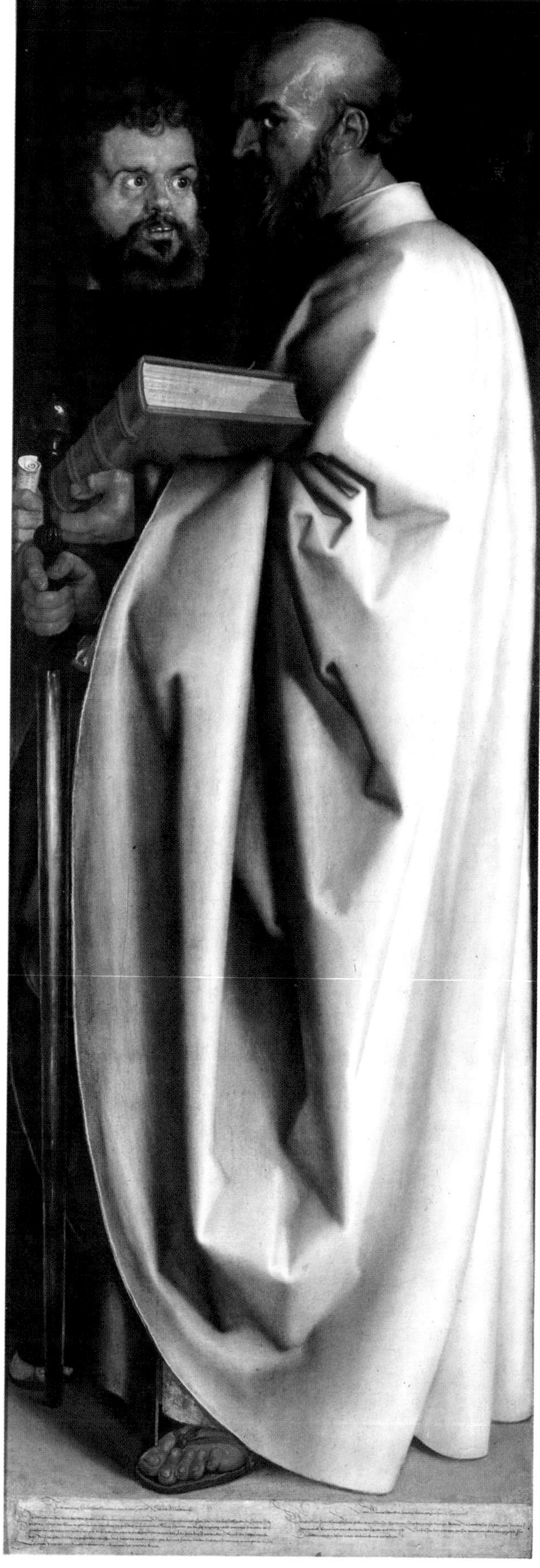

The Four Apostles. 1526. *"Painted with greater care than any other," wrote Dürer. This simple scene is his triumph as a painter. The massive figures fill the spaces majestically with their brilliantly colored, undetailed robes. In his old age, Dürer realized that the simplicity of nature was a true goal of art. The paintings glow from many coats of color applied over each other; he even formulated his own varnish. He gave the masterpieces to Nuremberg, inscribing below them the warning: "All worldly rulers in these times of danger should beware that they receive not false Teaching for the Word of God. . . . Heed, therefore, these four excellent men, Peter, John, Paul and Mark, their warning."*

Dürer 1471–1528

"ART SHOULD BE EMPLOYED in the service of the Church to set forth the sufferings of Christ and such like subjects, and it should also be employed to preserve the features of men after their death." These words express the attitude of Albrecht Dürer, a serious, religious man, and one of the most skillful artists of all time. Many consider him the supreme master of engravings and woodcuts. He was also a leading painter of the German Renaissance, working at the same time as the great Italian artists Leonardo da Vinci and Michelangelo.

Dürer was born in Nuremberg, the son of a goldsmith who wanted him to follow his craft, but who yielded to the boy's fine talent for drawing. Young Dürer became an assistant in a painter's studio when he was fifteen years old. In 1490 he set off to study in Germany, the Netherlands, and in Venice, a center of the surging art movement in Italy. His mission, he felt, was to learn all he could from the great painters and engravers of other centers. Dürer rapidly developed a complex but very precise style using highly detailed forms. The Italian artist Giovanni Bellini, admiring his work, asked to see the brush which produced such delicate lines. Dürer pulled one at random from a batch and painted a few thin, curling hairs to prove that his skill did it, not the brush.

The artist's fame spread. He wrote to a friend that one of his paintings made other artists so jealous that he could not attend the banquet of an artists' guild because he was afraid he might be poisoned. He was offered a lifetime pension if he would stay in Venice, but Dürer preferred his native Nuremberg.

He painted many powerful portraits, always striving for perfection of detail, and executed numerous series of woodcuts and engravings based on religious themes. Unlike the precision in most of his work, the sketchbooks of his many travels contain glorious watercolors—mostly scenes of the Alps—outstanding for their looseness and freedom of execution. It was not for three centuries that such superb watercolors were produced again.

Also a scholar of science and art theory, Dürer wrote books on anatomy, geometry, and painting. He produced many fine works, vigorous, detailed, and often accenting ugliness rather than beauty. A great master of the Renaissance, he set an example of supreme craftsmanship to inspire all artists.

Self-Portraits. 1484 and 1498. *When only thirteen years old, Dürer did the beautiful drawing above in silverpoint (using a silver stylus on specially prepared paper). In the oil painting below, one of many self-portraits, he showed a dandy of twenty-seven, pleased with his image in the mirror. Dürer's skill is clearly seen in details of the long curled hair, costume, and background of this elegant portrait.*

The Four Horsemen of the Apocalypse. About 1497–98. *As a master printmaker, Dürer refined woodcut technique (cutting lines into a block of wood, then printing from it) to the precision of metal engraving. As he had an extreme fear of death, Dürer filled fifteen prints of the* Apocalypse *(early religious writings) with horror and doom. This woodcut depicts War, Famine, and the Plague galloping over the world, with grimacing, skeleton-like Death in the forefront, crushing people under their horses' hooves. The imaginative prints were very successful, and sold all over Europe.*

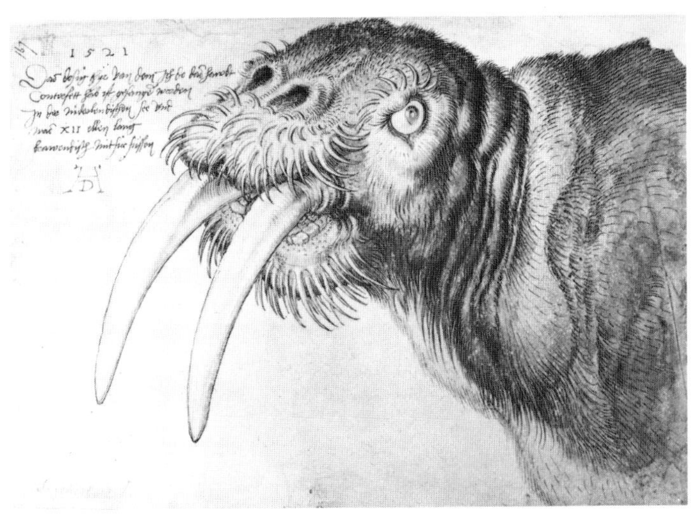

Nature Studies: Hare, Roebuck, Walrus, The Great Clump of Turf. 1502–21. *One reason for Dürer's superb craftsmanship is that he worked all his life for perfection in every detail. Seeking the truth in creation, he studied and drew animals, plants, birds, and insects. He drew each whisker and hair—even the tiniest pattern. Once he dug up a clod of earth, and painted a small masterpiece from it. His respect for nature's wonders shows in these marvelous studies.*

The Sistine Chapel Ceiling *(portion)*. About 1511–12. *This is a section of an almost unbelievable masterpiece covering over 10,000 square feet. The stirring Biblical themes on the ceiling, tracing the creation of the world and of man, contain 343 figures, 225 of them ten to eighteen feet tall. The scenes and the figures, including Old Testament prophets and Roman prophets or "Sibyls," are set in a huge network of marble columns, pedestals, and triangular and square frames, with many nude figures and huge gold medallions.*

The Creation of Man *(portion)*. 1511. *Just one of many panels in the Sistine Chapel ceiling, this is Michelangelo's expression of God imparting the gift of life to Adam by his touch, life flowing through his hand like an electric current.*

Michelangelo 1475–1564

"I AM DYING just as I am beginning to learn the alphabet of my profession," said Michelangelo Buonarroti on his deathbed, at eighty-nine. Sculptor, painter, architect, poet—many have called him "the greatest artistic genius who ever lived." A deeply religious, unhappy man, he felt that his art failed because no matter how good it was, it should be more perfect. He considered the human body a divine creation, and made most of his figures mighty beings with exaggerated gestures so they would be even larger, more powerful than in nature.

A moody boy, Michelangelo showed his talent early. From fifteen to seventeen, he lived as a guest in the palace of the noted art patron and ruler of Florence, Lorenzo de' Medici. When Lorenzo died, the young artist went to Venice and Bologna, then to Rome. He studied anatomy and dissected corpses to learn the body structure

Anatomy Sketches: Studies for the Libyan Sibyl. About 1510. *Michelangelo made many careful studies of anatomy. He drew the smallest details of the figure over and over again, to be able to reproduce perfect human bodies in his paintings. These studies in red chalk were for a figure on the ceiling of the Sistine Chapel.*

under the skin. He finished his first *Pietà* at age twenty-four, and his famous *David* at twenty-nine.

Throughout his life, strong rulers forced him to work to their orders, often against his own ideas and ideals. He hated having to paint so much of the time, for his real love was sculpture. Also, he was bitter about the wickedness of many leaders, and the general decay of morals. When Pope Julius II summoned him to Rome to create sculptures for his tomb, Michelangelo was delighted. He spent most of a year finding suitable blocks of marble. But the Pope changed his mind and ordered him to paint the ceiling of the Sistine Chapel instead. Michelangelo fled to Florence in 1506. Julius begged and threatened. In 1508, two years later, Michelangelo unwillingly started on the vast ceiling, and for four years he labored with superhuman effort. The result has been called "the greatest singlehanded work of art that man has ever produced." The poet Goethe wrote, "No one who has not seen the Sistine Chapel can have a clear idea of what a human being can achieve."

The key to the bursting form and energy in Michelangelo's paintings is his feeling that only painting which looked like sculpture was beautiful. He filled the Sistine Ceiling with many great, powerful figures which resemble enormous, life-like statues. At age fifty-nine, he was given an almost impossible task, this time an immense painting for the main altar wall of the Sistine Chapel, which he completed in seven years. The huge fresco, called *The Last Judgment*, filled with writhing nude figures of the damned, was attacked as a scandal. Michelangelo's last major commission was as architect for the magnificent Church of St. Peter in Rome, but he died, a lonely old man, before the dome was completed.

Pietà. 1498–99. *When only twenty-four, Michelangelo created this tender version of the Virgin Mother mourning over her dead son Jesus, in which he expressed his deepest emotions. The gentle gesture of her hand reveals unending sorrow, and she was made to look so young because, Michelangelo said, she possessed "eternal purity." Michelangelo's facility in handling marble is clearly revealed here; the hem of her robe is so thin in places that the light actually shines through. This is the only sculpture on which he put his signature, seen on the band across the Virgin's robe.*

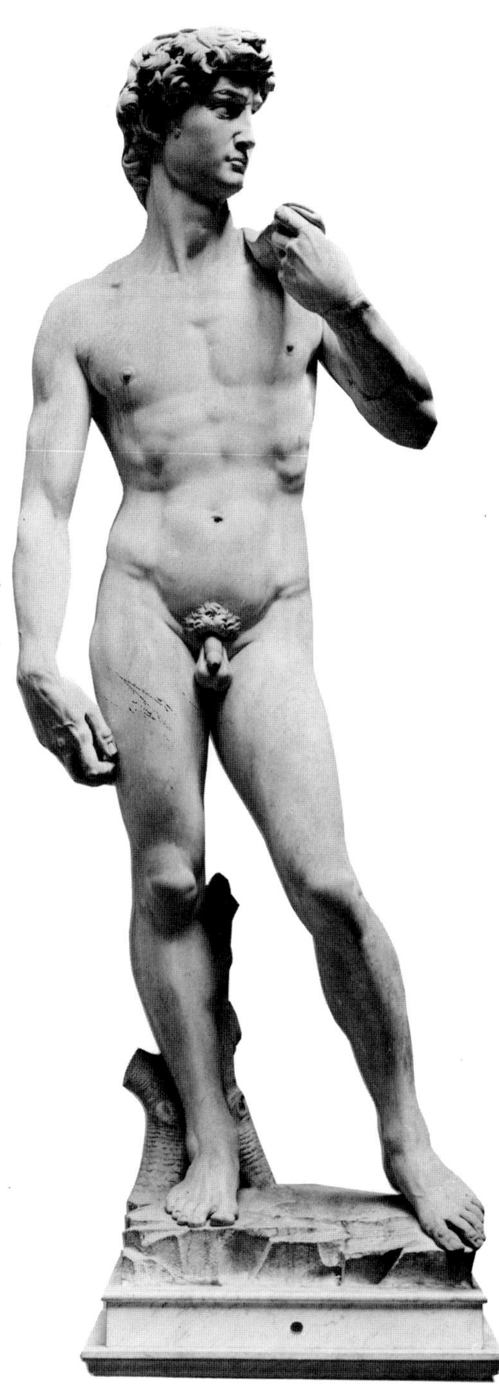

David. 1501–4. *The city of Florence gave the young sculptor, then twenty-six years old, a huge, misshapen block of marble that no one had been able to use. Michelangelo's vision, it is said, saw imprisoned in the stone the boy David, about to use a slingshot against the giant Goliath. Michelangelo was able to release the superb young body from its stone prison without even making any preliminary sketches.*

Florentine Pietà. About 1548–56. *How different this late work is from his* Pietà *of fifty-seven years earlier. It reveals Michelangelo's restless, tortured spirit in his eighties. The sorrowing head of Saint Joseph at the top is probably a self-portrait. He often worked on it at night by the light of a candle fixed in his cap. At one point, dissatisfied, he began to destroy the sculpture with his hammer, until his servant begged him to stop. It was repaired by an assistant. Though said to be unfinished, the sculpture is one of his numerous works that have a rough surface. Note how, in contrast with the highly polished first* Pietà, *this roughness, showing the lines made by the chisel, here acts as an expressive element to convey personal suffering.*

Raphael *1483–1520*

RAPHAEL (RAFFAELLO SANZIO) was the youngest of the three most famous artists of the Renaissance. He was strongly influenced by the other two geniuses of the trio, Michelangelo and Leonardo da Vinci. Yet there were great differences: Raphael was not fiery, moody, or strongly emotional, but was an elegant, sociable, sophisticated man. His personality is revealed in his art, graceful and poetic, filled with harmony.

Born in Urbino, a cultural center of Renaissance Italy, Raphael was exposed to fine works of art at an early age. His talent was soon recognized—when only about twelve years old he was given a place in the studio of the artist Perugino. Here he began to develop his style; throughout his life he sought to balance carefully all the forms in harmonious compositions, usually based on the form of a triangle or a rectangle.

At twenty-one he moved on to the very active artistic circles in Florence. There his work was soon highly praised, especially his paintings of the Madonna and Christ Child. In 1508 he went to Rome; a year later, Pope Julius II commissioned him to paint a series of frescoes on the walls of several new apartments in the Vatican Palace (at the same time that Michelangelo was working nearby on the Sistine Chapel ceiling).

In Rome, success followed success for the modest young artist. He painted portraits, sacred pictures, and frescoes, designed architecture, and made drawings for tapestries. Striving always to show beauty in harmony, he spread his interest widely, and took on too much work. When he hired assistants to hurry his work along, the paintings lacked the perfection that only Raphael himself could create. He was a master at combining soft, gentle colors and curving lines to create rhythmic designs and figures unmatched for their exquisite beauty.

But soon tragedy struck Raphael. Only thirty-seven years old, at the height of his career, the gifted artist contracted a fever and died. Fortunately he left a heritage of magnificent paintings for people to enjoy through the centuries—paintings which mark the high point of the Renaissance, the final goal of the search for the representation of perfect beauty and harmonious design.

Self-Portrait. About 1506. *Here Raphael shows himself as a sensitive young artist in Florence. Typical of his many portraits, this one is simple and elegant. The delicate edging of the white collar adds grace to the long neck, while the dark curving shapes of cap and suit harmonize with the soft eyes and hair.*

◀ OPPOSITE PAGE

Saint George Slaying the Dragon. About 1512. *Raphael painted this scene, one of two versions of the subject, when he was about nineteen. The painting, in oil on wood, is only $12\frac{1}{2} \times 10\frac{1}{2}$ inches. It tells the familiar story of the heroic knight on a white horse defending the lovely maiden against the wicked dragon. But Raphael's gentle colors and unity of figures and landscape make this a picture of calm beauty rather than of violence.*

The Casa Tempi Madonna. 1505–6. *Some of Raphael's most beloved paintings are of the Madonna and Child. In this masterpiece, painted in delicate blues, pinks, and greens, the sweet expressions and gentle curves convey the tender relationship of a loving mother and infant—the way Raphael thought of Christ and His Mother.*

The School of Athens. 1511. *Raphael's fresco, twenty-three feet long, on the wall of the Vatican Palace (the residence of the Pope), shows the ancient Greek philosophers, poets, and scientists grouped as if on a stage. See how he formed a large rectangle of the many graceful figures, set before rounded arches, to create an elaborate but unified, harmonious composition. It is believed that each of these figures was finished in a day. Many faces are portraits of contemporaries of Raphael, fellow artists or friends. The huge muscular figure in the center, pen in hand, was added after Raphael saw Michelangelo's work on the Sistine Ceiling; it shows how great an influence Michelangelo had on his work. In the detail, below left, we see the two central figures: Plato stands at the left, next to Aristotle—two of history's great philosophers. The bright archway attracts the eye and spotlights these men as the most important people in the crowd.*

Titian *About 1490–1576*

A Bacchanal (The People of Andros). About 1519. *In this exciting scene Bacchus, the Greek and Roman god of wine and revelry, finds the people of the island of Andros affected by drinking wine that flows from a brook. The turning, twisting motions of the figures give the scene exceptional vitality. The sheet of music at center bottom says: "He who drinks but once knows not what drinking is."*

TITIAN (TIZIANO VECELLI) has been called "the King of Portrait Painters." He showed his talent at an early age, and his parents soon sent him to Venice to study painting with the famous masters Gentile and Giovanni Bellini. He also came under the influence of a poetic artist named Giorgione, who died in 1510. In 1516 Titian was named Painter to the Republic of Venice, and soon established his personal style, which began a new era of Venetian art—the High Renaissance.

Titian's working process was revolutionary. Unlike his fellow artists in Rome and Florence, Titian did not make many preparatory drawings or concern himself with anatomical studies. Instead, he developed the process begun by his teachers of modeling his figures with layers of bright colors and subtle tones of light and shade. In other words, he did not draw with lines, but with colors. He would cover the canvas with a coat of red or white paint, and build up forms with a few simple strokes of another color. Then he would turn the canvas to the wall for a long time, often many months; later he would revise some forms, fill in others, and carefully finish the painting.

Almost all the important persons of his time wanted a portrait by Titian. Charles V, the Holy Roman Emperor, named him his Court Painter in 1533 and refused to be painted by anyone else. Pope Paul III and King Philip II of Spain also became his patrons. In his portraits Titian brought out the inner character of the sitter while still making him look thoughtful, handsome, and aristocratic. He painted richly figured fabrics and gleaming silks that seem so real that you want to reach out and feel them. The skin tones too seem very much alive.

In his later works, he applied masses of glowing color with increasingly free brush strokes, or more often with his fingers, to the amazement of his assistants. As a result his figures and forms seem to be blurred—they do not have any hard edges, but merge softly into the luminous background. Because these paintings broke away from tradition, they were not understood, and were criticized as "unfinished." Yet many of these loosely painted works, made in his last thirty years, are among his finest masterpieces. Certainly we see in Titian's style a beginning of modern painting, anticipating the loose brushwork of the nineteenth-century French Impressionists.

Self-Portrait *(portion)*. About 1562. *In this superb self-portrait of his later years, Titian revealed his own thoughtful and searching character.*

Portrait of Clarissa Strozzi. 1542. *This tender painting of a little girl feeding a pretzel to her dog reflects Titian's love for his own three children. It was recorded in the seventeenth century that it received great praise from the famous Spanish portrait painter Velázquez. The gay little cherubs on the base of the table appear also in some of Titian's many paintings of Roman gods and goddesses.*

The Entombment. 1559. *Titian painted this masterpiece when he was about seventy. It shows his remarkable ability to make colors vibrate in bright light and deep shadow. A glow seems to come from the mourning figures. Titian continued to paint magnificently right up to his death, when he was approaching the age of ninety.*

Saint Sebastian and Studies. 1520–22. *This painting of the saint who was shot through with arrows belongs to an altarpiece in the town of Brescia, Italy. At that time Titian was still composing pictures in traditional ways, and he may have made these sketches to show his patrons what he intended to do. They are rare examples of his drawing. Note how in each one Titian sought to bring out the tortured movements of the body, to express suffering through the loose, swiftly drawn lines.*

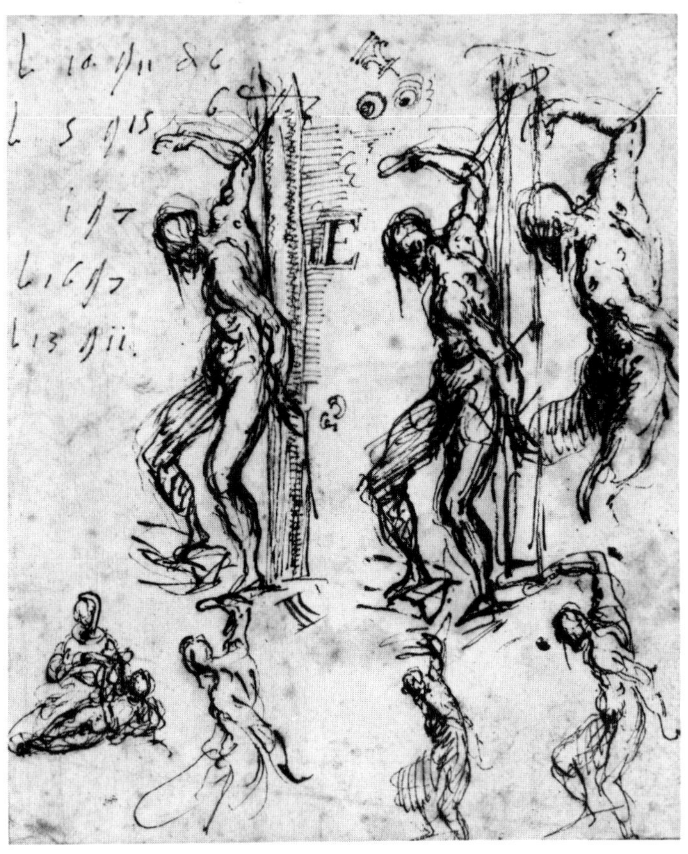

Henry VIII. 1540. *Holbein painted this very powerful King of England to look as solid as a stone wall, filling the picture with his massive body. This is hardly a flattering portrait, for it reveals every feature, including the small, tight lips and hard, commanding eyes. Yet the huge body and magnificent robes produce an awe-inspiring effect. Also, Henry's rigid pose, one hand squeezing the gloves, the other clenched, shows him as the one and only authority. The amazing exactness of every bit of fabric, jewels, and other items establishes Holbein as a master of detail as well as characterization.*

Holbein *1497–1543*

HANS HOLBEIN THE YOUNGER and Albrecht Dürer were the most important German artists of the Renaissance, although Holbein spent most of his life in Switzerland and England. He became perhaps the greatest painter of realistic portraits in northern Europe.

Holbein was born in Augsburg, Germany, the son of an artist. His early training was in his father's workshop. By 1515 he had gone to Basel, Switzerland, with his brother Ambrosius. Soon he was a successful artist, making many woodcuts and engravings for printers, as well as painting frescoes, portraits, and religious scenes. He may have visited Italy about 1517, for in his work after this period he combined northern European attention to detail with the solid, monumental forms found in Italian Renaissance art. Three portraits of the scholar Erasmus of Rotterdam, which he painted in 1523, made Holbein famous. As an accomplished portrait painter, he aimed in each work to portray the sitter only and exactly as he looked to the eye. Holbein's art was honest to the point of harshness, as he shunned sentimentality.

At that time northern Europe was being torn apart by the religious Reformation. In Basel as well as in Germany, followers of the reformer Martin Luther banned religious paintings and sculpture, stating that people were thus led to worship images of God instead of God himself. As the conflict made it difficult for Holbein to paint, he went to England in 1526 with letters of introduction from Erasmus. "Here," wrote the scholar, "the arts are shivering. He [Holbein] is going to England to pick up a few coins."

Holbein painted portraits of Sir Thomas More, Chancellor to the King, during his first visit. He returned to Basel, but left again for England in 1532. In London there were few English painters of any merit. King Henry VIII soon appointed Holbein as Court Painter, the post he held until his death. In this new position Holbein made designs for goldsmith's work and architectural decorations, as well as many paintings, in lifesize and miniature, of Henry and his family (including several of his six wives), and the royal court. He was even sent to other European countries to paint portraits of royal women whom Henry might wish to marry.

Today, Holbein's portraits and other works endure for their solidity, honesty, and craftsmanship. His pencil and brush probed every detail of a sitter's features so faithfully that not only the subject's likeness but his character came through clearly.

Study for a Self-Portrait. 1542–43. *This drawing, made with colored chalks on pink paper, is a study for a self-portrait. In the eighteenth century the drawing was enlarged on all sides, as you can see, and was painted over with watercolor and gold. The uncompromising clarity with which Holbein revealed himself has not been lost.*

Edward VI as Prince of Wales. 1538. *One of several Holbein portraits of Henry's only son, this was presented to the king on New Year's Day, 1539. It is a clean-cut likeness of the royal baby, tender but not sentimental. Note how the boy's features resemble his father's, but with dramatic contrast between the innocence of the child and the worldliness and strength of the man. The inscription in Latin begins: "Little one, imitate thy father . . ."*

Family of the Artist. 1528–29. *This scene of the artist's family, painted on paper pasted on wood, has been called "the most beautiful picture of the German School." Holbein portrayed his wife and children accurately but with affection, revealing the cares and sorrows of their lives. The wife, once beautiful but now sick and grief-stricken, holds the children tenderly. This intimate but mercilessly realistic scene is perhaps Holbein's finest portrait.*

Erasmus of Rotterdam. 1523. *This revealing life-like portrait is one of the three that Holbein made of the great scholar and author. The artist's superb talent at portraiture makes us sense the powerful, searching mind of Erasmus.*

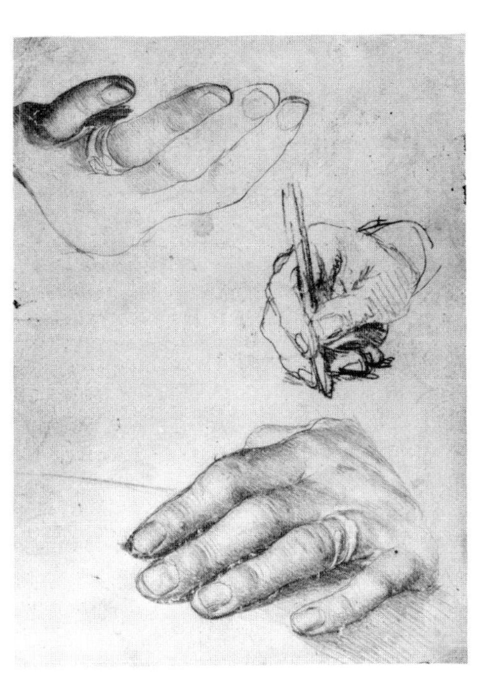

The Hands of Erasmus. About 1523. *Before and while painting his portraits of Erasmus, Holbein made careful studies such as these fine drawings of the sitter's hands.*

The Peddler. 1523–26. *This brilliantly designed woodcut, shown in its actual size, is one of many in Holbein's imaginative series* The Dance of Death. *It shows Death taking the lives of those he chooses, whether good or evil. Here Death overtakes a peddler, who argues that he must get on with his work of selling the goods on his back. With sensitive lines Holbein made drawings to be copied by engravers onto wood or metal; prints were then made from the plate.*

Summer: The Harvesters. 1565. *Following an old custom of calendar illustration, Bruegel painted six known "seasons" pictures, which were deservedly popular. In* The Harvesters, *hot sunlight shimmers through golden fields. The haze of heat vibrates into the pale sky, making distant areas almost disappear. He set the horizon high up to fit in a vast landscape view, and held everything solidly together by using the tall tree as a backbone. His people are real, whether hot and wearily at work, eating in the tree's shade, or sprawled in sleep.*

OPPOSITE PAGE ▶

Winter: Hunters in the Snow. 1565. *In dramatic contrast,* Hunters in the Snow *conveys the chill of wintry silence in every detail—the heavy, lead-gray sky with no sense of sun, skeletal, bare trees, weary, hunched-over hunters with their subdued, shivering dogs, and figures huddled over a fire. The sharp descent of the hill to the skating ponds provides a dramatic entrance to a vast landscape, leading to the icy mountains far away. Bruegel also created distance with diagonal lines one behind the other, pushing back into space. The patterns of snowy white and dull greens bring harmony everywhere.*

Bruegel *About 1525–1569*

No artist has ever surpassed the genius of Pieter Bruegel the Elder in bringing crowds of people alive in paintings. He pictured people so vividly that we seem to be right there with them. He not only captured the spirit of peasants working, snoring, playing, or stuffing themselves with food, but also used crowd scenes almost as an excuse for creating landscape backgrounds of breathtaking vastness and beauty.

Born in an area now part Holland and part Belgium, by age twenty-six Bruegel was already a master of the Painter's Guild in Antwerp. From his journey to Italy in 1552–53, he brought back superbly detailed landscape drawings, mostly of the Alps, from which he gained ideas for later paintings. In some masterworks he combined Alpine scenes with Flemish settings.

Well educated, Bruegel was an original thinker and creator, not a follower. While artists around him were painting in Italian Renaissance fashion, Bruegel invented his own style. Using live models, he made countless sketches which helped him place hundreds of little figures beautifully in a limited space. With skillful use of the brush he painted strong, flat colors right next to

each other. He gave figures roundness and weight through adept drawing and color variety rather than with light and dark tones. His pictures have a wonderful balance, each figure, shape, and color harmonizing in a fine, intricate all-over pattern.

Bruegel drew only what appealed to him. He never painted a portrait, for example. He created fresh versions of Biblical themes, picturing not exalted figures but sturdy working people. He was well known and admired in his day, mostly for widely sold engravings based on his paintings. In these seemingly innocent scenes of peasant life, Bruegel subtly included satirical comments on the political and religious conflicts which were going on around him. There is a story that late in life he painted pictures revealing quite openly his rage against religious persecutions, along with biting caricatures of important persons. These are said to have been lost because, on his deathbed in Brussels at the age of forty-four, he ordered his wife to burn them, fearing that they would cause her and the family serious trouble. Yet many masterpieces remain, re-creating for us the lusty peasants and glories of nature he loved best.

The Wedding Dance. 1566. *A master of crowd action, Bruegel filled this painting with such vitality that you can almost hear the shouts, laughter, and stomping of shoes. Brightly colored curving shapes dance through the picture, adding to its gaiety. Bruegel went to many country festivals to study the stocky peasants, and earned the nickname "Peasant Bruegel."*

The Blind Leading the Blind. 1568. *Bruegel liked subjects which point a moral, here a New Testament story: "And if the blind lead the blind, both shall fall into the ditch." Bruegel was probably saying that those who followed evil leaders would get into trouble. Against a quiet, gentle landscape setting Bruegel has created a dramatic composition of the row of groping, sightless figures, the followers almost frozen with fear as they feel the leader stumbling into the ditch. Yet they too stumble on, unable to prevent their own fall.*

The Triumph of Death *(detail)*. About 1562. *This painting clearly shows the influence on Bruegel of Hieronymus Bosch, a Dutch artist who created weird creatures of the imagination. This small detail of a nightmarish scene shows both rich and poor being overpowered by Death's terrifying army of skeletons. You must look carefully at this painting to see the many fantastic, exciting scenes all taking place at once.*

THE SAVIOUR. About 1604

These pictures of Christ and two saints are clearly the visions of a most devout man. The hands are gentle, the faces exalted. The warm brown colors, the strong contrasts of light and dark tones, and the lively brushwork make the images glow as if bathed with a kind of heavenly light. El Greco set his figures against a dark background, concentrating on them alone. Although he made the head and hands long, slender forms, he gave the holy figures strong, powerful bodies which he emphasized by clothing them in voluminous robes.

El Greco *1541–1614*

SAINT JOHN THE EVANGELIST. About 1604

SAINT LUKE. About 1604

"MY SUBLIME WORK," El Greco called his religious paintings, which express a spiritual feeling unlike any other in history. The stretched heads and elongated figures seem pulled upward to the sky. Some critics once claimed that the odd, lengthened "El Greco look" was due to faulty eyesight, but this theory is not held today. In some of his portraits, such as *Don Fernando*, there is little distortion. El Greco purposely exaggerated his figures as part of the expression of his very personal style and because he considered them "heavenly bodies which appear larger in the same way as lights seen from afar."

Domenico Theotocopoulos was born and raised on the island of Crete, now part of Greece; later he was called "El Greco," or "The Greek." He received his early training in Crete, where the artistic styles (including rich colors and stiff, unreal forms) of the Byzantine Empire of previous centuries still flourished and influenced him. El Greco went to Venice, where he may have been a pupil of the great master, Titian. There he learned the importance of color in modeling figures. About 1577 he went to the city of Toledo, an artistic and intellectual center of Spain, where he lived for the rest of his life. A sensitive, cultured, devout man, El Greco spoke many languages, had a large library, and was a friend of eminent Spanish scholars and writers.

During the terrible Spanish Inquisition, El Greco developed his strange, passionate, and disturbing art in the sixteenth-century trend known as Mannerism. This was a style in which artists, primarily Italian, broke the "rules" of the Renaissance period of the fifteenth and early sixteenth centuries. Instead of creating balance and harmony in a perfectly proportioned composition, as Raphael had done, artists purposely distorted or exaggerated the human body, emphasized the unimportant details of a scene rather than the central theme, reorganized perspective, and used harsh, vivid colors. They sought to shock the viewer and achieve emotional effects.

With the years, El Greco distorted his figures more and more, and emphasized dramatic features: angular patterns, flame-like flashes of light, sharp-edged draperies, exaggerated expressions and gestures, and eerie colors. His late works show increasing violence and passion. King Philip II of Spain rejected his work and El Greco never became a success at court.

Supposed Self-Portrait. About 1600–10. *A few years before his death El Greco painted this sad portrait, possibly his own likeness. The time-worn, ashen face was also used as the model for the painting of Saint Luke—the saint who was supposedly an artist.*

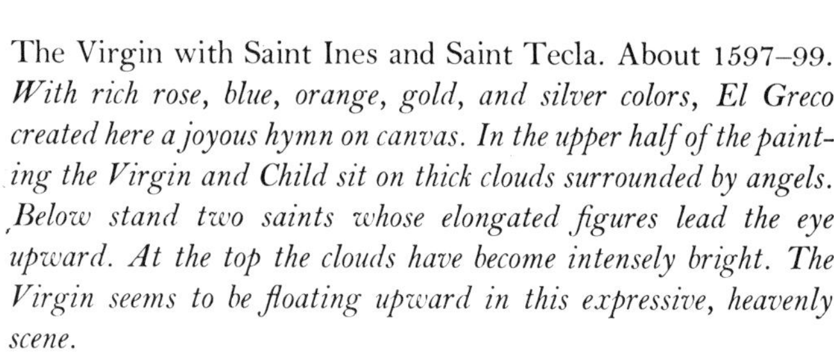

The Virgin with Saint Ines and Saint Tecla. About 1597–99. *With rich rose, blue, orange, gold, and silver colors, El Greco created here a joyous hymn on canvas. In the upper half of the painting the Virgin and Child sit on thick clouds surrounded by angels. Below stand two saints whose elongated figures lead the eye upward. At the top the clouds have become intensely bright. The Virgin seems to be floating upward in this expressive, heavenly scene.*

Portrait of Don Fernando Niño de Guevara. About 1600. *This cardinal, known as "The Great Inquisitor," caused much bloodshed and misery. But El Greco has created a sad portrayal of a man torn apart by the conflicts of good and evil. The right hand is relaxed; in contrast, his left hand is clenched rigidly under the flaring cape. El Greco has used a glorious red to set off the costume of the cardinal from the brown background.*

View of Toledo. About 1604–10. *This scene, one of the most beautiful and dramatic landscapes ever painted, shows the town of Toledo huddling under the threat of violent storm clouds. El Greco could see Toledo from the windows of his workroom, and used parts of the view as background in various works. He loved painting the groups of buildings on the steep, rocky hills that were bordered by a winding river.*

Rubens *1577–1640*

Wolf and Fox Hunt. About 1615. *This is a superb example of Rubens' genius in combining active figures and elements of all sizes and shapes in a unified, harmonious design. Everything is exciting and full of life; note how the center of the scene is filled with the snarling animals and the rough, powerful huntsmen, in violent contrast to the controlled and seemingly cool, aristocratic portrayal of the couple on horseback.*

Rubens and His First Wife. 1609–10. *Every detail of the texture and patterns of the splendid clothing of this handsome, devoted couple is perfect—such naturalism was traditional in Flemish painting. The fullness of color and warmth of feeling, however, could come only from the hand of Rubens. The artist's left forefinger points to the caressing hands as if he is saying: "Look, we are joined as one."*

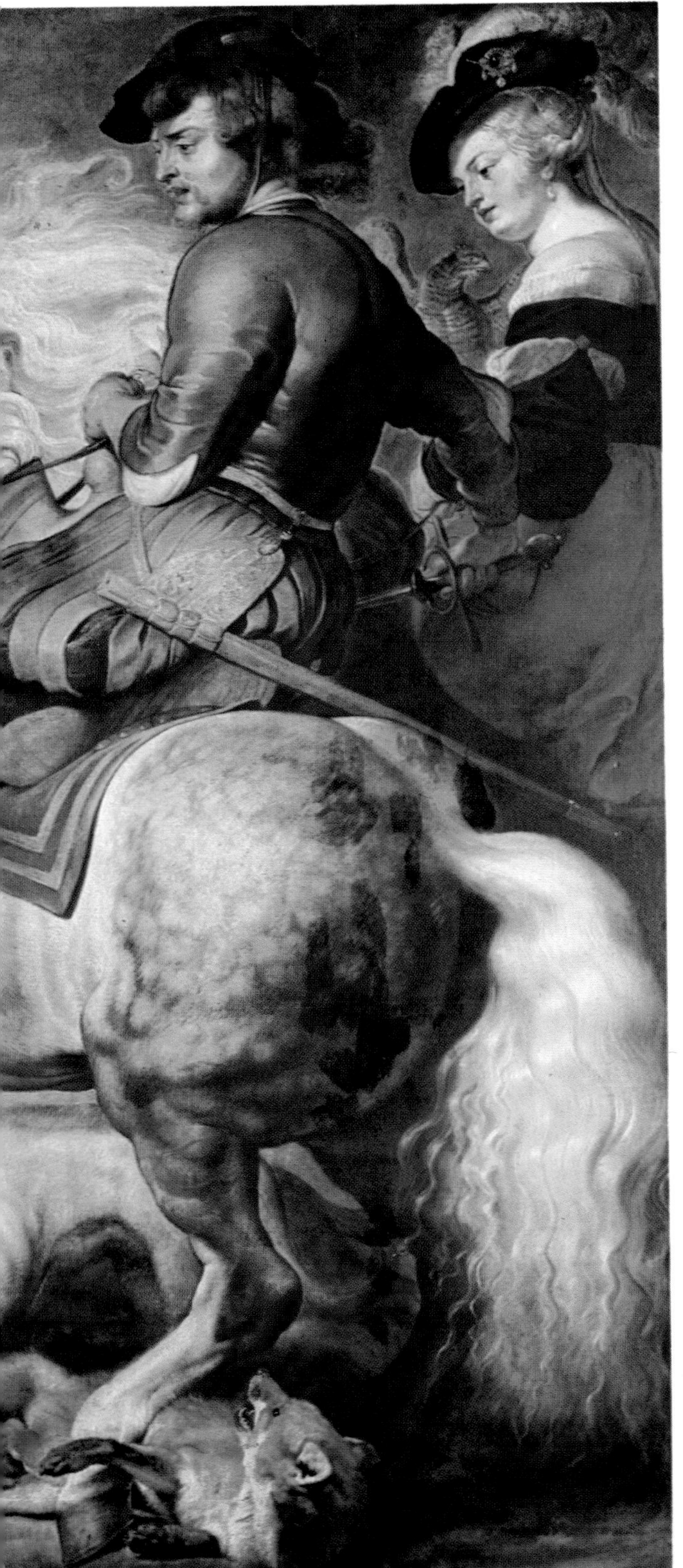

"NO UNDERTAKING, however vast in size and diversified in subject, ever daunted my courage," said Peter Paul Rubens, the greatest Flemish artist of the Baroque era. This statement was not an empty boast, but a fact of his strong character and personality. Rubens completed more than fifteen hundred paintings, many of which were enormous and filled with dozens of twisting, turning figures. Although he used numerous assistants, his genius alone inspired every work.

At age fourteen, Rubens knew he wanted to be an artist. After nine years of studying art, during which he also learned six languages, he went to Italy. There he stayed for eight years as Court Painter to the Duke of Mantua. Rubens gained much from Italian art, particularly from the work of Titian and Michelangelo. In 1608 he returned to Antwerp, where he was made Court Painter to the Spanish conquerors of Flanders. For the palace of the Queen of France, he finished twenty-four huge pictures.

Rubens earned a great fortune from his art. He lived in a mansion with his wife, eight children, horses, hunting dogs, art galleries, fountains, and glorious gardens. Yet he worked long, exhausting hours, often arising at four o'clock to catch all the daylight possible. He succeeded as a diplomat, too, and was sent on missions to Holland, Spain, and to England, where he was knighted by King Charles I.

While most Flemish and Dutch painters of his time stayed with one type of subject matter, Rubens tackled anything except still life: religious, mythological, and battle scenes, nudes, studies of children, portraits, and landscapes. A highly adaptable, inventive artist, he created rich color variations, light-and-dark effects, and powerful, curving figures noted as "Rubenesque." Although each painting was carefully planned and perfected down to the tiniest details, the canvas was made to vibrate with his rapid brushwork and shimmering flesh tones, at which Rubens is unsurpassed. His masterpieces are as fresh and lively today as when created over three hundred years ago.

The Artist's Sons, Albert and Nicholas. 1624–25. *Rubens' love and pride in his sons is revealed in their elegant dress, shining faces, and confident poses. The attention of the younger son, Nicholas, then about six or seven years old, is fixed on the fluttering bird tied to a string. Albert, a few years older, holds a book and dangles a glove like a man of the world.*

Studies of Cattle. *Evident here are Rubens' drawing skill and love for nature and its fascination. You can sense his pleasure in searching with his pencil for the muscle and bone shapes, and the twistings and turnings of the animals on their short, knobby legs.*

The Adoration of the Magi. 1624. *This huge masterpiece, about eleven by fifteen feet, is one of many of Rubens' religious pictures praising the glories of the Church. Here he used a typical Baroque composition, in which the forms are arranged so that they seem to go back into the depth of the scene along imaginary diagonal lines, running from corner to corner and meeting in the middle. On these lines are placed the lively forms of men and animals, directing our eyes to the Virgin and Christ Child at right. The robust bodies and radiant flesh tones are typical of Rubens' style. He painted earlier versions of the Adoration with many more figures, but here he simplified the scene to create a powerfully emotional effect. Look at the variety of faces—of many different ages and origins—and the wonderful heads of the camels.*

Frans Hals

1580–1666

Self-Portrait. About 1650. *Here the artist's eye is more probing, revealing clearly how time and trouble have lined and changed his face. Note how simple his composition is, how quiet and restrained the pose. Hals could not have been unaware of Rembrandt's searching self-portraits. Compare these works with the six self-portraits by Rembrandt.*

"VITALITY" IS THE BEST DESCRIPTIVE WORD for the paintings of Frans Hals, one of the most famous artists of the Baroque period of art in Holland. He is popular throughout the Western world for his portraits of laughing people. A master at handling brush and paints, he was able to capture a laugh, a gesture, or a sparkling eye, and fix it on canvas forever.

Happy-go-lucky Hals did not usually penetrate a subject's character as did his contemporary, Rembrandt, for Hals lacked his poetic vision and searching curiosity. But when you view one of his pictures today, more than three centuries later, the person still seems vividly present. A laughing Hals print on the wall is like having a merry companion in the room.

In Haarlem, Holland, a scholarly teacher named Karel van Mander, who knew the art of other countries, passed on his knowledge to the young painter. Hals was also influenced by his great Flemish contemporary, Rubens, who visited him in 1624. Hals' technical ability was supreme, each brush stroke sure. His paintings glow with rich blacks, silvery grays, and subtle whites; and the skin tones are in bright tones of red, pink, and yellow.

CONTINUED ON PAGE 66

Portrait of a Man and His Wife. 1621. *During a prosperous period Hals painted this couple, thought to be a portrait of himself and his second wife, in rich silks and a lavish setting—typical of fashionable portraiture of the time. Note his remarkable talent in highlighting the precisely painted white lace of the collars and cuffs against the darks of the silk clothing and foliage. How different this picture is from his lively, free paintings of lusty barroom characters.*

Yonker Ramp and His Sweetheart. 1623. *Hals captured the gay gestures of a young couple in this colorful painting. Here we see his mastery in creating warm, even flushed, skin tones. The brushwork is rapid and skillful. The artist designed the picture brilliantly, in a typically Baroque manner: he made a diagonal leading from the man's upraised right arm, to his sweetheart's hand, down to his left hand under the dog's chin. In this way a lively composition is created, and the viewer is made to follow these lines into the depth of the scene, so he will see the warm fire and the laughing servant.*

The times were prosperous, so portraits were in demand. Hals became a very successful, fashionable painter of wealthy citizens. For his own pleasure, in the taverns where he passed the time, he swiftly sketched noisy companions and troubadours strumming guitars, lifting glasses, or singing drunkenly. Hals had more than eight children, and five of his sons became artists. He made money painting and teaching, but lived lavishly and spent his earnings recklessly.

As he grew older the demand for his work declined. In his eighties, Hals lived poorly on a small pension given him by the city of Haarlem—where he spent almost his whole life—as a token of the fame he had brought there years before. Long after he died, his laughing faces and fine portraits won him a lasting place in the history of art.

Boy with a Skull (*sometimes called* Hamlet). About 1625–28. *At that time portraits were often posed with skull in hand, perhaps to show the link between life and death. It is not likely that Hals was portraying Hamlet, the hero of the tragic play by Shakespeare, as this is not a usual stage costume. Note how a few simple strokes with Hals' superb brush turned the feather in this hat into a masterpiece of fluff.*

The Women Regents of the Old Men's Home in Haarlem. 1664. *This solemn picture of the governing board of the local poorhouse, painted when Hals was in his eighties, marks a deeply tragic period in his life. He himself was poor and depended on a small pension to survive. The work is dark and somber, with little color in the thin faces, which seem to stare at us so sternly yet kindly, or in the old, worn hands. In this and other late works Hals, partly because of his own sufferings, sought to show the character and humanity of his sitters.*

Velázquez *1599–1660*

Self-Portrait. 1656. *Velázquez painted himself at work in this detail from* The Maids of Honor*—a dark, handsome member of the court. He was then fifty-seven years old.*

DIEGO DE SILVA Y VELÁZQUEZ, painter of royalty, was the outstanding Spanish artist of the Baroque era, and one of the world's greatest portraitists. He began his art studies at thirteen; using a peasant boy as a model, he drew him in hundreds of different poses. Some of Velázquez' early paintings of peasants showed a lusty freedom that was later refined in formal court studies. He worked hard to develop his natural ability for painting portraits, and soon was able to portray a sitter accurately.

When Velázquez moved to Madrid at twenty-four, he painted the portrait of a court official, which immediately became so popular that King Philip IV ordered his own portrait. The result was also such a success that the king appointed the young artist as Court Painter, gave

CONTINUED ON PAGE 70

Prince Balthasar Carlos on Horseback. About 1634. *Born in 1629, King Philip's first son was a fine rider; here Velázquez portrays him astride his pony. The warm browns and pinks of the proud prince and his mount stand out against the cool colors of the sky and the countryside.*

Prince Balthasar Carlos. About 1640–42. *This last formal portrait of the prince, who died shortly thereafter, features Velázquez' rich and varied handling of blacks. Note how the braided design on the clothing is echoed in the furniture. The curves of the arms, silver strap across the chest, and black cape lead our eyes to the pale face.*

The Infanta Margarita. About 1653. *The silver and pink designs of the dress, the rug patterns, and the vase of lovely flowers all relate to each other in a beautiful, simple design. The Infanta, or princess, daughter of the second wife of King Philip IV, is like a lovely little flower—shy and pretty.*

The Infanta Margarita. About 1656. *At about age six, the princess looks like a small queen doll. Velázquez brought out her wistfulness even in this magnificent court costume. Margarita remained Velázquez' favorite subject, and he died leaving his last portrait of her unfinished.*

The Infanta Margarita. About 1655. *In this more formal portrait, at age five, the child is growing fast out of babyhood, as if she knows she is preparing to be a queen. In fact, she became Empress of Austria when she was fifteen. The flowing, golden hair harmonizes with the braiding, bracelets, and ribbons.*

Prince Felipe Prosper. 1659. *Velázquez tenderly showed the frailty of the two-year-old baby in contrast with the perky, sprawling puppy on the chair. The deep reds of the painting surround the little pale figure and thrust him forward out of the deep shadows. Felipe died two years later, leaving the throne without an heir.*

him a large living allowance, and ordered all earlier portraits of himself removed from the palace. Through the years Velázquez painted the king many times, as well as the royal family, other members of the court, attendants, dwarfs, and buffoons.

Besides portraits, Velázquez created stunning works such as the *Surrender of Breda*—a panorama of men at arms with prancing horses and far-flung landscape—and the *Tapestry Weavers*—a brilliant scene of women and colorful cloths and tapestries. The Spaniard made several trips to Italy, and in 1650 painted two exquisite landscape views, seen from a Roman villa. They rank among his finest works. Velázquez' paintings were triumphs of dramatic simplicity, never crowded with cluttering details. He would purposely use a plain background in order to make the figure stand out.

Even while seeking to please the king and the court, Velázquez tried not to flatter but to reveal the inner person in each portrait. He always attempted to represent the truth as he saw it in his sitters. His portraits of the king's children, especially, live on as masterpieces of color, design, and beauty.

King Philip IV at Fraga. 1644. *This is a superb example of Velázquez' handling of bright colors placed against a simple dark background. His genius at design is shown in the costume's graceful decorations—the silver, white, and red tones repeat in varied patterns like the themes of a symphony.*

Surrender at Breda. 1634–35. *One of the finest historical works of all time, this magnificent painting celebrates an important Spanish victory—over the Dutch city of Breda. On a hill overlooking the burning city, and surrounded by the troops with their tall lances, the victor is graciously telling the defeated leader that he should not kneel as he presents him the key to the city. The strong horizontal mass of the figures is balanced by the repeated verticals of the weapons. Velázquez quite daringly placed a sleek brown horse in the foreground with the major figures, in perhaps his most beautifully and perfectly designed painting.*

The Maids of Honor (Las Meninas). 1656. *Velázquez has created a masterpiece that is a triumph of light and shadow. We see him standing before a huge canvas—he is painting the portrait of the king and queen, who are reflected in the mirror behind him. The Infanta Margarita and her attendants (maids of honor), dwarf, and dog have come to watch her parents being painted. Thus Velázquez has cleverly varied the usual scene in which he sets the little princess.*

SELF-PORTRAIT. About 1656

Rembrandt used himself as a model for more than sixty self-portraits. As with his portraits of others, each one is a scrupulously honest rendering, yet there is much sympathy and understanding. Rembrandt achieves the effects of age by building up the face in layers of pink and tan skin tones, highlighted with strokes of thick white paint, and deepened with soft brown and dark red lines. He also creates an exciting, slightly mysterious atmosphere by clothing the figures in dark, voluminous robes that seem to melt into the surrounding shadows; in contrast, the face is bathed in a warm, glowing light that comes from an unseen source.

SELF-PORTRAIT. 1629

SELF-PORTRAIT. 1650

Rembrandt 1606–1669

ART EXPERTS OFTEN HAVE DIFFERING OPINIONS about a painter's work, but most of them are in agreement on one point—that Rembrandt was one of the greatest artists of all time. His art is unmatched for the depth of sympathy, insight, and compassion for people that is found in his work.

When Rembrandt painted a portrait, the result was far more than a fine likeness; it was a work of art in every way. Through the masterful design, details of expression and form, and the glowing lights and deep shadows, Rembrandt was able to probe deeply into the personality of the sitter, to reveal the individual's inner character and, some say, even his soul. Almost no artist before or since the time of Rembrandt has handled contrasts of lights and darks as well.

Rembrandt van Rijn was born in Leiden, Holland, the son of a miller. He revealed his talent early, drawing from the time that he could use a pencil. He studied art in Leiden and Amsterdam, and when only twenty-four opened his own studio in Amsterdam. There he spent the remainder of his life. His work was liked from the start, and his first group portrait, *The Anatomy Lesson of Dr. Tulp*, made him famous.

Yet Rembrandt was not easily satisfied. He experimented with techniques and designs, but his advances

SELF-PORTRAIT. 1659

SELF-PORTRAIT. 1660

SELF-PORTRAIT. 1663

Rembrandt CONTINUED

Jacob Blessing the Sons of Joseph. 1656. *A deeply religious man, Rembrandt painted many scenes from the Bible. As he grew older, the artist's sympathies for people deepened. His paintings became more simple and expressive, with larger shapes, broader areas, and fewer details. Note how the faces, filled with light, in contrast to the dark shadows, convey the drama of this moment, as do the tender gestures of the hands. We feel the love and closeness of the family as the aged grandfather reaches out, with support from his son, to bless the small boy.*

were too different from the usual art of his time to be easily understood and accepted. As he grew more skillful in the use of light and shadow, and created fewer elegant, supposedly naturalistic portraits, many patrons turned against him. When the determined artist painted sixteen members of the Amsterdam Musketeers in *The Night Watch* in 1642, he was severely criticized. The painting was denounced as not accurately representing the face of each member, and as being much too dark.

Rembrandt's life became increasingly difficult. His business declined, his beloved wife Saskia and three of his four children died, and he became bankrupt in 1656. Weak, almost blind, he went on painting masterworks which will live forever. Altogether he produced over six hundred oil paintings and almost two thousand drawings and etchings.

The Polish Rider. About 1655. *Whatever subject Rembrandt painted, the result was masterful and gripping. This handsomely costumed rider radiates youthful boldness and vitality as he poses astride his high-stepping horse. The brilliant handling of light makes this pair stand out from the dark, loosely painted landscape. The picture has an expectant air, hinting that there is adventure to come for this wandering soldier.*

A Cottage among Trees. About 1648. *Rembrandt's warm appreciation for the beauty of nature is revealed in this simple landscape scene. Through sensitive lines and shadows he contrasts the feathery, waving trees with the low, dark roof of the barn. He re-creates for us the peaceful loveliness of the countryside in his time. Rembrandt was one of the world's greatest masters of both drawing and etching.*

Vermeer *1632–1675*

Supposed Self-Portrait. 1656. *The man in this detail from an inn scene is believed to be Vermeer at twenty-four. The artist pictured himself as a pleasant-faced, shy young man quietly enjoying the company of friends.*

JAN VERMEER (JOHANNES VAN DER MEER) is famed for his "quiet" masterpieces. There are no still-life pictures by him, but he treated every subject like a still life. Each individual form and figure appears to be solid, calm, fixed in a beautiful tableau. He painted interior views masterfully, though he did not always tell a story or seek to arouse emotions.

There is a magic quality about the warm, glowing light that floods Vermeer's paintings. His colors have a purity and clarity never before achieved in art. The exquisite tones placed delicately together absorb and radiate light. With his rare pictorial vision and skill, he created absolute beauty out of the most commonplace objects. He transformed ordinary domestic scenes into an art of simple elegance.

Vermeer was born in Delft, Holland, a center famous

CONTINUED ON PAGE 78

A Young Woman with a Water Jug. About 1660. *The decorative window appears often in Vermeer's interiors. The source of light was always a very important and beautiful element of the design to him. It is said that the young woman is about to water plants outside the window—indeed, the whole painting has an air of suspended motion. Note how skillfully Vermeer has rendered the silver jug and bowl—surely one of the most beautiful details in all art—so that they reflect the bright sunlight and mirror the objects nearby as well. You can see the blue cloth reflected on the side of the jug, and the red patterned rug on the bottom of the bowl.*

OPPOSITE PAGE ▶

The Artist in His Studio. About 1666. *The artist at the easel may be Vermeer. All his rare talents contribute to this masterpiece, a perfect example of Dutch interior painting. In spite of the many details, the effect is of stillness and order. Bright sunlight flooding the room brings out graceful shapes and shadows. The exquisitely painted drapery in front acts like a theater curtain, and places the figures back in the studio. The wonderfully detailed chandelier, the map with every crease showing, the beamed ceiling, and the tiled floor—all these add up to a design of supreme artistry.*

NOVA XVII

for the manufacture of lovely porcelain. Some people think his surroundings caused his work to have a "porcelain look." When he was twenty-one he joined an art guild. Later he became an art dealer as well as an artist, but could not sell his own paintings. Buyers who were interested in dramatic subjects and portraits preferred other Dutch artists whose work was more lively and more warmly realistic. Yet although critics of the time did not appreciate the poetic color and harmony in Vermeer's peaceful pictures, he went on painting in his own way.

His art-dealing business was never profitable. Though burdened by money troubles, supporting his wife and eleven children with difficulty, Vermeer painted his greatest works between the ages of twenty-eight and thirty-eight. Five years later he died suddenly of an unknown cause. It was not for another two hundred years that his paintings—only thirty-six are credited to him today—were acclaimed as among the finest ever created.

A Lady Reading a Letter by a Window *(detail)*. About 1658. *One of Vermeer's favorite subjects was a woman reading or writing letters. This woman may be Vermeer's wife, who, it is believed, often posed for him. In this typical early work the light moves from the window, illuminates the letter, hands, and face, highlights the hair, and then flows over the figure to the wall behind. We can see on the sleeves and hair the beginnings of his development of the little "pearls" of light which later became typical of his style.*

A Street in Delft. About 1660. *At first glance this carefully designed painting looks like a photograph. The many varied shapes of the roofs are contrasted with the curved arch of the door at the left, and with the figures of women and children. Vermeer has recorded his observations of this outdoor scene in every detail; he may even have seen this view from his studio window.*

The Kitchen Maid. About 1658–60. *In this golden picture, Vermeer used the full scale of luminous yellows against the cool blues and greens of an apron and a tablecloth. The maid looks calm and detached as she goes about her duties. The objects on the table form a lovely still life, while the milk pouring from the jug has the glow of porcelain. Light from the window radiates beauty throughout the picture.*

Gainsborough

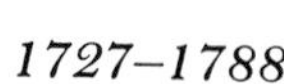

1727–1788

Self-Portrait. About 1758–59. *Gainsborough portrayed himself as a handsome, aristocratic young man of just over thirty. Following his usual style, he used a modified landscape background.*

THOMAS GAINSBOROUGH, the famous English portrait painter who really loved doing landscapes, often skipped classes in order to sketch the countryside. Once he gave his teacher a false note stating: "Give my son Tom a holiday." His angry father said: "That boy will be hanged!" Then he saw the drawings Tom did that day, and exclaimed: "That boy will be a genius!"

Gainsborough emerged from an interesting background in English art. Until Anthony van Dyck came from Antwerp in 1632, there was little native English painting. Swamped with demands for portraits, Van Dyck filled his studio with assistants and pupils. That led to the Golden Age of English art—the eighteenth century—which produced a number of fine artists. But Gainsborough surpassed them all in his ability to create both superb portraits and landscapes.

At thirteen Gainsborough went to London for eight years of art training. He worked hard, and slowly started to sell his paintings. In 1759 he moved to Bath, where rich and famous people vacationed. There he found many who desired portraits. He said that an artist "may do great things and starve in a garret if he does not conquer his passions and conform to the common eye in choosing

CONTINUED ON PAGE 82

Robert Andrews and His Wife. About 1750. *This charming couple, placed in a country setting, is a fine example of Gainsborough's early portraiture. He studied the facial features carefully, and created exceptional likenesses. The pose of this country gentleman and his wife is also very natural, unlike the aristocratic formality of most of his later portraits. Many of these included beautifully painted feathery trees, green fields, and cloudy skies.*

The Watering Place. About 1777. *Gainsborough's love of English landscapes is evident in this masterwork. Friends told how Gainsborough often created landscapes by setting up what he called "thoughts." He would place on a table some small stones, dried herbs, and bits of mirror, which became rocks, trees, and water in pictures. Sometimes he used broccoli for trees. He made tiny animals and figures, and then painted them in large landscapes—he even brought live animals into his studio as models. Although* The Watering Place *was perhaps his finest landscape, he still owned it at his death because there was no demand for "pure" landscape painting, or scenes that did not tell a story.*

that branch which they will encourage and pay for." So, although he preferred painting England's lovely scenery, he created fashionable portraits in order to make a living. He included scenery in many of his portrait backgrounds, but his landscapes did not sell.

A success at forty-seven, he moved to London, where members of the royal court and society sought to be painted by him, although many preferred to sit for his rival, Sir Joshua Reynolds. Unlike Reynolds and other artists of the time, Gainsborough painted all his works himself, without any assistants. Because of his love of painting, he labored to create fine pictures as well as good likenesses. His increasingly skillful, sensitive brushwork and inventive color produced enduring art.

During his last eight years he often painted for his own pleasure, creating sentimental country scenes of peasants, children, and animals. These story-telling "fancy pictures," as they were called, soon became popular. Years after his death, the noted English artist John Constable said about Gainsborough's gentle landscapes: "On looking at these paintings, we find tears in our eyes, and know not what brought them."

OPPOSITE PAGE ▶

The Honorable Mrs. Graham. 1775–76. *Lush, fashionable portraits like this one were no challenge for Gainsborough. He painted his subjects glamorously, making them look as though they had descended from a long line of aristocrats. The richness and elegance of the fabrics and the large-scale, imposing setting reflect his study of portraits by Van Dyck, Rubens, and Italian masters.*

Blue Boy (Jonathan Buttall). About 1770. *The very famous, appealing* Blue Boy *was painted when Gainsborough was most popular. The figure stands in a usual "studio-portrait" pose, in clothes of bright colors against a softly painted landscape. The artist's ability and delight are seen in the play of brushwork, swirling in the rhythms of the hat's feather, the trees and clouds, and the wrinkles of the silken clothing. It has been said that Gainsborough painted the costume in bright blue simply because his rival, Reynolds, told his students that it was a most difficult color to use well.*

Goya 1746–1828

Self-Portrait in a Tall Hat. About 1826. *Painting himself at age eighty, in spite of deafness and near blindness, Goya reveals his alertness and spirit in a few broad, still vigorous brush strokes. Dressed in finery for the portrait, he peers out at the world with a mysterious, haunting smile.*

FEW ARTISTS IN HISTORY lived through such horrors as did Francisco de Goya y Lucientes He expressed his agony in many paintings and etchings which give us a deeper understanding of Spanish life and history.

During his eighty-two years he produced about five hundred oil paintings, almost three hundred prints, and one thousand drawings. He was a master of the traditional styles of portraiture, yet at the same time he was a daring experimenter. His approach was frank and truthful, and his works cried out against injustice.

Born in a poor village in northern Spain, he began to study art at fourteen. By 1766 he was working for the Painter to the King of Spain, and he later married this master's sister. Goya visited Rome, returned to his home in Saragossa, then went back to Madrid about 1775. There he obtained work in a tapestry factory, making paintings which were used as designs—called "cartoons"—by the weavers. During a period of seventeen years Goya made sixty such paintings, which provide a colorful picture of the more charming aspects of Spanish life in his day. At forty he was appointed Court Painter to King Charles IV. His portraits of the royal family and court immediately became famous, but surprisingly so, for although dressed in magnificent costumes, the figures were unflattering likenesses, clearly revealing any physical ugliness and weakness of character.

When he was forty-eight Goya was stricken with a severe illness that left him deaf. His unofficial paintings, even more than before, became charged with emotion, and his brushwork became increasingly free and vigorous. In 1798 he completed the frescoes for the ceiling of the Church of San Antonio de la Florida in Madrid, in which he actually used sponges instead of brushes to apply the dabs of color, and thus created beautiful, loose forms rarely seen in art at that time.

When the French invaded Spain in 1808, Goya's deepest feelings were roused. He had hoped that Napoleon's army would bring needed reform against enslavement of the masses; instead there was terrible slaughter. Goya depicted his horror in some of the most stirring etchings ever created, the series called *The*

CONTINUED ON PAGE 86

Don Manuel Osorio de Zuñiga. 1784. *This appealing painting reveals Goya's tenderness and love for children. Notice the loving, careful treatment given even to the shiny satin and delicate lace. Like his predecessor Velázquez, Goya often painted his subjects, beautifully clothed, with only a few broad strokes of the brush. Then he set them against a dark background in order to make them stand out. This portrait glows with the innocence of the child, who is unaware of the cats' eager interest in his pet bird.*

Disasters of War. In his paintings his brush seemed to drip with blood; it was said that after the execution of some patriots by a firing squad, he actually dipped his handkerchief in pools of blood and on a wall outlined the design for his powerful painting *The Executions of May 3, 1808, in Madrid.*

Many of his paintings of protest were done on wall panels in his home, Quinta del Sordo (Deaf Man's House). Unable to bear the oppression in Spain, in 1824 Goya went to Paris, then settled in Bordeaux, where he lived in exile, deaf and almost blind, until his death four years later. His work has affected art through the ages.

The Executions of May 3, 1808, in Madrid. 1814–15. *Man's inhumanity to man had probably never been pictured so starkly before. In an agonized reaction to the atrocities of war, Goya portrayed the brutality and horror of an execution in Madrid. The use of fiery colors and a blazing light in the dark night centers all our attention on the helpless victims, especially the man with raised arms, and on the pool of blood. In contrast to the fear-stricken faces of the victims, the executioners—Napoleon's troops—are presented as a row of anonymous, well-dressed soldiers, intent only on carrying out their orders.*

Two Old People Eating Soup. 1820–22. *Again sick at seventy-three, Goya plunged into a frenzy of work. Slashing away like a madman, he covered the walls of his home with fourteen nightmarish scenes called the "Black Paintings," one of which you see here. Frantically, from the visions of his tortured mind, he created these dark, lurid, unearthly scenes. He once said that fantasy and imagination had no limits as far as his paintings were concerned. He distorted, exaggerated, and intensified forms and colors in a remarkably free manner. He is supposed to have said that he could not see lines in nature, but only the masses, shadows, and reflections of light.*

And There Is No Remedy (*from* The Disasters of War). Begun 1808. *In this monumental series of eighty-three etchings, Goya depicted with each forceful line the deadly suffering inflicted on the Spanish people by the French invaders. Goya's aim was to show man's dignity, goodness, hopes, and joys being shattered by evil, leaving only agony and despair. Compare this with his monumental painting of the* Executions of May 3 . . ., *where he has depicted the same firing line and the twisted corpse.*

Burning of the Houses of Parliament. 1835. *This masterpiece was begun the night the Houses of Parliament burned to the ground in London. Turner rushed to the scene, horrified and entranced by the soaring flames. He dashed out one version after another of the fantastic scene, filling fifteen pages in two watercolor sketchbooks. This painting—done almost entirely with a palette knife instead of a brush—sums up his vivid impressions of the drama of flames bursting into the black sky, intensified by the reflections on the water of the River Thames.*

Turner 1775–1851

Self-Portrait. About 1798. *Young Turner, already praised for his Romantic pictures, portrayed himself with handsome, large eyes and a poetic expression. How strikingly different this painting is from the free, exciting works he made many years later.*

Joseph Mallord William Turner, one of England's greatest artists, was accused in his time of "flinging a pot of color in the public's face." Born in a dingy area of London, son of a barber, he was soon recognized as a child prodigy. He began formal art study at the Royal Academy at fourteen, showed his watercolors a year later, and was hailed for his oils when only twenty. He was thirty-three when appointed Professor of Perspective at the Academy. Later he traveled to Europe, then visited Rome and Venice several times, making many sketches.

Turner's early works were Romantic in the popular style of the day when an artist was supposed to show nature exactly as it looked, not imposing his own viewpoint. The pictures sold well, and Turner could have been very successful painting what the eye sees. But as he traveled, grew older, and thought more deeply, his attitude changed. In his last thirty years especially, he made creative discoveries about light and its relation to color that have influenced painting ever since, preceding the Impressionist movement in France.

He loved to paint boats and the sea, trains puffing steam, bridges and mountains, particularly as they were affected by nature's violence—wind, snow, rain, or fire. Art critics attacked his less detailed, more imaginative paintings. They said that parts of his pictures were like "blots," that his sea looked like "stone," that his waves were "chalky." A famous artist of his time, John Constable, called Turner's work "Airy visions, painted with tinted steam." Defiant, Turner departed from strict reality even more.

Usually he did not paint right from the subject, but spent days making rough pencil sketches, lines and shapes appearing and vanishing. Then he added colors from his memory and personal inner vision, in swirls and soft-edged forms. If he used figures at all, they became smaller, practically lost in his re-creation of nature and dazzling light. People called his work "unfinished," but he shrugged it off and kept painting. Some days he would tramp up to twenty miles even in the stormiest weather, absorbing nature, then sketching rapidly. He was one of the most productive of artists—more than nineteen thousand drawings were found in his studio when he died at seventy-six.

George IV at a Banquet in Edinburgh. 1822. *In the 1820s Turner became interested more and more in figure subjects. In 1822 he traveled to Scotland to record the state visit of King George IV. The king is but a golden blur at the head of the long table. The crystal chandeliers are barely visible overhead. The loosely painted figures seem to stretch endlessly into the background, giving the impression of an enormous banquet. The individual elements have been subdued for the total effect, though there is a lovely still-life scene on the table at left.*

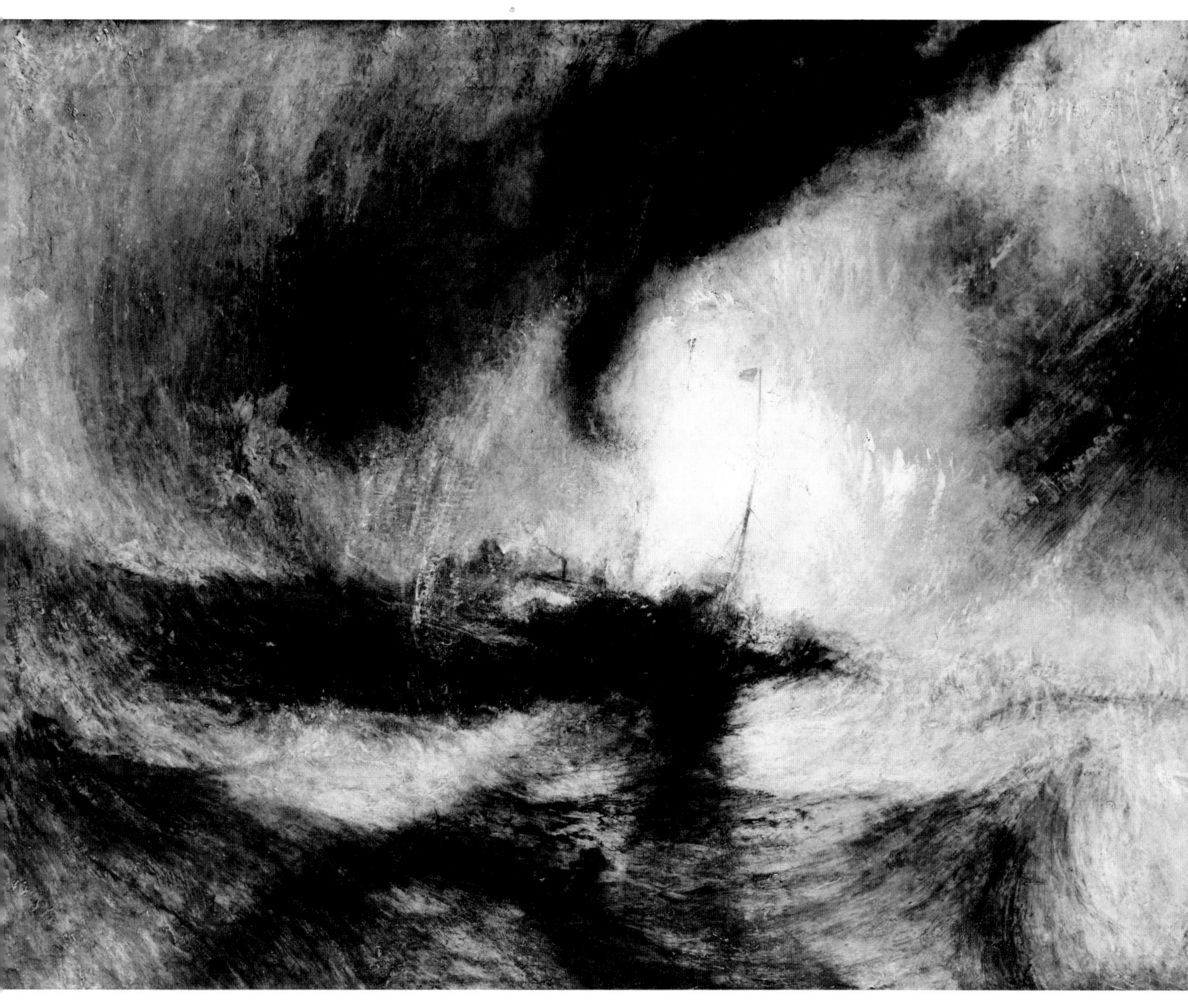

Snow Storm. 1842. *Here Turner was portraying a real event, as indicated by his complete title for this painting:* Snow Storm—Steam-Boat off a Harbour's Mouth Making Signals in Shallow Water, and Going by the Lead. The author was in this storm on the night the Ariel left Harwich. *During the raging storm he persuaded sailors to lash him to the mast for four hours. In grave danger he watched the storm swirling about him as in a devil's whirlpool. Later he said: "I did not expect to escape, but I felt bound to record it if I did." Realism and his artistic vision merge. Looking at the painting, you feel that you are right in the center of the storm, for everything—boat, sky, and water—rushes around in one great swirling movement.*

◀ OPPOSITE PAGE

San Giorgio from the Dogana, Venice: Sunrise. 1819. *This watercolor, only about nine by twelve inches, expresses Turner's poetic reaction to Venice. You feel as if you are on the scene catching the first glow of sunrise, which he has recorded so sensitively—with delicate washes of color he captures the reflections on still water, boats at rest, and the graceful outlines of the Venetian Church of San Giorgio.*

Delacroix *1798–1863*

Dante and Vergil in Hell *(detail)*. 1822. *Delacroix used his imagination and genius to bring to life scenes from the writings of Shakespeare, Byron, Scott, and others. Aroused by Dante's famous* Divine Comedy, *he had a friend read the work to him as he painted "like a madman." Striving to capture this drama on canvas, Delacroix—then in his early twenties—said that he had found himself as an artist. He derived the large, muscular, writhing figures from his studies of Michelangelo; compare this scene and the Sistine Chapel ceiling.*

"IF YOU ARE NOT SKILLFUL ENOUGH to sketch a man jumping out of a window in the time it takes him to fall from the fourth floor to the ground, you will never be able to produce good work." This advice, from Eugène Delacroix to a student, shows Delacroix' passion for painting scenes of action so that they seem to be taking place before your eyes.

Delacroix broke away from the rigid tradition of his early training to paint freely and emotionally. Most of his pictures are filled with action, with bold, swinging brush strokes loaded with strong reds, blues, and other vigorous colors. His style became known as "Romantic" painting. With Delacroix at its head, the movement influenced art throughout the nineteenth century.

Born near Paris, the son of a diplomat, Delacroix later knew poverty and loneliness. His mother's death when he was sixteen crushed him, as he noted in a letter: "I cannot see what I am writing for tears." He plunged into art and never let up. He studied Rubens and other Old Masters; he said that the ideal art would be a combination of the styles of Michelangelo and Goya. Visiting England, he was inspired by the bright colors of the landscape painters Constable and Turner. Everywhere he sketched, studied, and painted.

Delacroix used many historic, religious, and literary themes, trying to make each picture *say something*—to make people feel, not just to please them. Some of his works are like story illustrations by a master artist, full of violent, exaggerated gestures and flaming colors. He could express joy or suffering with a few sweeping lines. Because he loved the beautiful movements of

Self-Portrait. 1837. *The burning spirit of the artist painting his deepest emotions shines through here. Most of his portraits reflect strong personal feelings, because they were of people he knew and liked, such as his friend Frédéric Chopin, the great composer.*

Women of Algiers. 1834. *Enchanted by Algerian women, Delacroix sketched them at their daily activities. Back in Paris, he painted this typical scene so vividly that you can almost smell the incense. His eyes noted the tiniest details of color and design, which his hand brilliantly preserved for us. The rich interweaving of colors in such scenes as this one would inspire Impressionist painters years later.*

Massacre of Chios. 1824. *The painting's full title was:* Scenes of the Massacre at Chios: Greek Families Awaiting Death or Slavery. *A critic denounced this masterwork as "the massacre of painting," because its turmoil was so different from calm, classical pictures. Sickened by the slaughter of twenty thousand Greeks on the peaceful island of Chios during the Greek-Turkish War, Delacroix studied all the historic details, making countless sketches for seven months. Then he filled a huge canvas (almost fourteen by twelve feet) with the despair of the suffering victims. The painting won an award and was bought by the French government, marking Delacroix as the leader of the new Romantic movement.*

Delacroix CONTINUED

animals, Delacroix spent time at the zoo and elsewhere sketching tigers, lions, horses, etc. He became one of the greatest animal painters, able to make his fighting, snarling, leaping beasts seem alive. At age thirty-four he traveled through Morocco, Algiers, and Spain. The colors and violent contrasts of North Africa inflamed his work. He filled seven sketchbooks with action-packed drawings which he used as subjects for paintings.

In spite of recurring fevers and sickness, he would not rest, saying: "I have enough work for another four hundred years!" When he died at age sixty-five, the writer Silvestre summed up: "So died, almost smiling, Delacroix, painter of the first order, who had a sun in his head and storms in his heart, who for forty years played upon the whole keyboard of human passions, [with a] grandiose brush, now terrible, now gentle. . . ."

Head of a Roaring Lion. About 1843. *This fierce, life-like watercolor portrait of a lion reveals why Delacroix has been called one of the greatest painters of animals the world has ever known. His rapidly applied brush strokes catch the expression so vividly that we can almost hear the king of beasts roaring.*

Horse Attacked by Panther. About 1825. *Few artists in history could capture an instant of violent action as Delacroix did in this watercolor, a whirling scene of snarling, fighting animals.*

Arab on Horseback Attacked by a Lion. 1849. *This dramatic picture again combines some of the subjects Delacroix liked best to paint: a violent lion and a rearing horse in the swirling dust. With the addition of rich, dazzling colors, this scene shows us an exciting view of African life in Delacroix' time.*

Daumier 1808–1879

"HE WAS OF THE PEOPLE and he loved people from the bottom of his heart," said a friend of Honoré Daumier, whose art has been compared to Rembrandt's for compassion and Michelangelo's for vigor.

Born of a poor family, at thirteen Daumier worked as an errand boy in a Paris court. He saw so much suffering in his youth that for the rest of his life he fought against injustice with bitter, revealing drawings, lithographs, paintings, and sculpture. The overworked youngster, set on being an artist, spent every spare minute drawing. He copied the works of the Old Masters in the Louvre Museum. In his late teens he went to art classes. Clerking in a book store, he would pore over prints and lithographs to absorb and learn all he could.

Since there was no photography then, newspapers and magazines depended on drawings. Daumier's career began when he sold some cartoons to the journal *La Caricature.* His art attacked all who mistreated the masses. In 1832, when his cartoons ridiculed the unpopular tyrant King Louis Philippe, Daumier was fined and sentenced to six months in jail. Released from prison, he again fought social evils with his pen. A new law made political caricature a crime in 1835, so Daumier invented comic characters and situations which gave a vivid picture of his time. Though he yearned to paint and sculpt, low pay kept him at his drawing board.

Whenever possible, Daumier painted oils and watercolors of his beloved working class, as well as studies of the circus, theater, and other subjects. They were not "pretty pictures"—he aimed to rip aside pretense and show raw emotions. His style became increasingly free: simple, but powerful. He re-created details from memory and imagination rather than from live models. But his paintings were liked only by a few friends.

At age fifty-two, this quiet, honest man was dismissed from his job. Burdened by poverty, he still created some of his finest paintings and sculpture. He was rehired in 1864, and made enough money to live. However, again penniless, and losing his sight by the time he was sixty, he was about to be thrown out of the little house he rented. A good friend, the artist Camille Corot, bought the house and gave it to Daumier as a gift. There the embattled artist, practically blind, died at seventy-one. An exhibition arranged by friends a year before had won some critical approval, but little else. Soon after his death his works were sold to dealers for very low prices. Like Rembrandt, whose art he loved, Daumier was too far ahead of his time to be appreciated fully while he lived.

Self-Portrait. About 1853. *Unhappily, Daumier could not afford materials, and made little sculpture. He molded faces and figures with the same intensity we see in his paintings. Here he reveals himself in plaster as sensitive and stormy-browed.*

OPPOSITE PAGE ▶

Don Quixote. About 1868. *Daumier often painted the idealistic, slightly mad hero of fiction who "fought windmills" with a spindly spear, astride a bony horse. The contrast between Don Quixote's noble dreams and his pitiful failures probably reminded the crusading artist of himself. His tones had been mostly soft reds, browns, and greens, but now he moved to brighter colors. He covered thick layers of light paint with transparent dark colors, creating an unusual glow. See how the stark landscape adds to the unreal mood and gives dramatic importance to the ghostly horse and rider.*

The Laundress. About 1860–62. *From his Paris home near the River Seine, Daumier saw washerwomen toiling daily. Here he painted a mother wearily carting a heavy, wet bundle and helping her child, who carries the paddle used to beat the clothes. The strongly expressive figures, like sculpture in their fullness of form, show the artist's sympathy for working people. His use of large masses of blacks and whites in drawings led to similar effects in his paintings.*

Two Sculptors. About 1863–66. *With swift and sure brush strokes, Daumier built up these figures on the surface of a small piece of wood (eleven by fourteen inches). He created form with layers of bright colors, very much as these sculptors modeled their clay. The fresh, sketchy quality gives an air of intense excitement to the picture.*

Circus Parade. About 1865. *This is a sketch for a watercolor in the Louvre Museum, Paris—a masterpiece of movement and superb draftsmanship. Every line surges with action so that we seem to be there, hearing the trio's cries. We feel Daumier's compassion for the sadness behind the exaggerated gestures and grimacing faces of the clown, animal trainer, and fat lady.*

Manet *1832–1883*

IT IS SAID THAT MODERN PAINTING began with Edouard Manet, for he freed his work of the unrealistic, overly sentimental subject matter of his time. He painted life as he saw and felt it—as it appealed to his *senses.* He portrayed his friends, from all levels of society, without disguising them in religious or mythological scenes. Even more important was his technique: he stopped using *chiaroscuro* to create shadows. Instead, he painted bold colors side by side, producing strong contrasts of forms in clear, bright light. His work caused much argument in his time, and was rejected by the public. But Manet was a revolutionary—his techniques and free choice of subjects were an inspiration for the Impressionist movement then beginning in France.

Manet never meant to be controversial, for he was a charming, cultured man and wanted only to be accepted in the official Salon in Paris. His well-to-do parents had been opposed to his becoming an artist. In 1848 he sailed on a merchant vessel for South America, to begin a career in the navy. But after the voyage, Manet knew what he wanted to do, and turned to studying art with an established master. At the Louvre Museum in Paris he made many careful copies of works of the Old Masters Titian and Velázquez; their influence (which you can see by comparing the portraits of each by these artists) remained with Manet throughout his career.

Although Manet was a revolutionary artist, in the

CONTINUED ON PAGE 102

Self-Portrait with Palette. 1879. *Note how Manet's brushwork has loosened in this late painting. We can see how obviously he made his coat, brush, beard, and hand of simple broad strokes of brown and yellow paint—we are as conscious of the brush strokes themselves as we are of the forms they create. Manet did not choose to reverse his mirror image, so he appears with the brush in his left hand.*

Race Course at Longchamp, Paris. 1864. *Manet made many studies of this Parisian race course in 1864: watercolors, oil paintings, and a lithograph. In this exciting version, in oil, the horsemen are rushing toward us, right to the edge of the canvas. The perspective is sharply defined by the fences alongside the track. With a skillful light hand, Manet created the spectators, trees, and hills with short, broad strokes of bold blues and greens and pale pinks.*

Don Mariano Camprubi. 1862. *Colorful Spanish subjects appealed to Manet. He painted the dancer, Mariano Camprubi, in Paris, in a very personal way. He formed dramatic contrasts of color by using a white costume, red cloak, and black background. The stage floor, a simple area of gray with dark areas denoting shadows, is used for design rather than realism, and helps bring everything forward.*

Manet CONTINUED

formation of his style he drew upon many sources: the Old Masters, the more recent work of Goya, Daumier, Delacroix, the art of Japanese prints (for their bright colors, bold outlines, and simple forms), and the very new art of photography. Manet was also influenced by the Impressionists to paint more freely and bring more light into his colors. He produced some of his finest boating scenes while working with the Impressionist Claude Monet (and made a drawing of Monet, which is reproduced on page 114). Manet painted a wide range of subjects: still lifes, portraits, cafés, picnics in parks. His visit to Spain inspired many scenes of bullfights, ballet dancers, and beautiful women.

Through many years of controversy, few of his works were accepted by the Salon and the public. His two greatest works, *Luncheon on the Grass* and *Olympia*, aroused public wrath. They were considered scandalous and vulgar because of their frank portrayal of nude women.

In his forties, a paralyzing sickness struck Manet. Attacks of illness weakened him so that he could not stand at his easel. He went on working, often using pastels, for they were easier to handle. Manet died at fifty-one, leaving over four hundred oil paintings, one hundred watercolors, about eighty-five pastels, and many prints. Said Degas after Manet's funeral: "He was greater than we thought."

A Bar at the Folies Bergère. 1881–82. *Manet finished this beautiful painting a year before he died, when he was seriously ill. He loved to paint scenes of Parisian night life. A friend who watched Manet at work on this painting said: "Although he painted from life, Manet did not by any means copy it; I realized his great gift for simplification. . . the tones were lighter, the colors brighter. . . . The whole formed a light and tender harmony." The background behind the bar is a mirror, but he has altered the reflection for design rather than realism. In the reflection, the back of the bar maid is seen far on the right, and she is listening to a man whom we do not see at all in front of the bar!*

Portrait of Emile Zola. 1868. *Zola, one of a group of writers and artists with whom Manet met often, and who always defended his work, wrote: "We may laugh at Manet, but our sons will go into ecstasies over his pictures." This painting was influenced by Manet's study of Japanese prints, with their black lines and flat color areas. Note the reproduction on the wall of a Japanese print next to Manet's famous painting* Olympia, *and behind it a copy of the painting* Bacchus *by Velázquez. At the left we see part of a Japanese screen. This portrait was denounced by a critic who said: "The accessories are not in perspective, and the trousers are not made of cloth." Of course not—the trousers are made of* paint. *Manet wanted us to be aware of this, because pictorial means, particularly his brushwork, were as important as the subject.*

Boy with a Fife. 1866. *This famous painting is quite simply formed of areas of color, without shadows or modeling. Notice that the background seems as close to us as the boy, but there is a feeling of roundness in the figure, created by the broad, bold brush strokes of dark colors against the area of gray.*

Degas *1834–1917*

EDGAR DEGAS IS FAMOUS for his pictures of ballet dancers and horses. His art has been called "beauty in motion" because, even though fixed on canvas or paper, his figures seem to be *moving*. Much of the time he directed models in his studio to keep moving around as he made "snapshot sketches" with amazingly swift strokes of his pencil.

Born in Paris of a wealthy family, Degas never had to worry about money. Enjoying the arts and going to museums was part of his childhood. In his early twenties he started copying the works of the Old Masters. From his study of the work of the great French painter Ingres (1780–1867), he learned how to model the figure. Japanese prints inspired Degas to draw strong lines, and to sketch scenes and people from unusual angles. He kept going to the theater, ballet, and racetrack to sketch musicians playing, dancers bending and kicking, and horses running—always *action*. He worked to capture this sense of movement in oil paintings, pastel drawings, and sculpture.

In spite of praise for his superb drawing and design, Degas was never satisfied. He would seldom sell his pictures. When he did, he would try to borrow them back—and then never return them. His feelings of doubt, and nagging worries about his failing eyesight made him seem mean and unfriendly. Once he looked at a young artist's work on exhibit and turned away, saying: "I am sorry for you!" Yet he helped many others, including an American, Mary Cassatt, who became well known for her paintings of mothers and children.

In his last five years, Degas was almost totally blind—he saw only shadows, if anything. He groped his way around Paris, where he had spent most of his life, until he died at the age of eighty-three.

The Dancing Class. 1880. *Degas liked best to use pastel crayons, as here, so that he could draw and color at the same time. In his late oil paintings, he painted with lively strokes, as if using pastels.*

Frieze of Dancers. About 1885–90. *In this painting, Degas used large, simple forms and airy colors. The dancers (the same model in four different poses) have a rare beauty, like swaying flowers in a field.*

Before the Performance. 1882–83. *Degas' dancers, painted with sensitive lines and fresh colors, seem to float like yellow and orange butterflies. Their legs and arms form a pleasing design with the trunks and branches of the trees.*

Four Dancers and Scenery. About 1903. *This is a fine example of Degas' pastels. His eyesight dimming, he showed few details. He brought the background and figures together by repeating the curving lines of the costumes and scenery. By cutting off part of the dancer at right, Degas produced the effect of a photographed scene rather than a posed picture. Photography was then becoming popular, and influenced many artists.*

Self-Portrait. 1855. *This sensitive etching shows an already moody Degas at age twenty-three.*

Race Horses at Longchamp. About 1873–75. *Degas loved to look at horses and paint their grace and movement. Here he has pictured the activity before a race in an exciting pattern of horses and riders in sunlight and shadow.*

The Glass of Absinthe. 1876. *This is Degas' best-known painting of people in Parisian cafés. It caused a scandal when it was exhibited in London, as it was taken to be a shocking picture of the evils of drinking. However, Degas was really trying to present an impersonal portrait of two lonely people—the models were two of his friends—sitting in a café. The design is exciting and daring; note how the lines zigzag, starting from the bottom of the canvas and running across the table tops. The design was inspired by the Japanese prints which the artist greatly admired.*

The Little Fourteen-Year-Old Dancer. 1880. *Degas started to sculpt in his thirties, in order to learn about the forms of horses and people. Some fifteen years later, he fashioned this lovely dancer in wax. He used real fabric: satin shoes and bodice, and tulle skirt, all coated with wax. As his eyesight became worse, he sculpted more often than he painted, since his fingers could feel what his eyes could not see.*

The Blue Vase. 1883–87. *In this masterpiece, Cézanne achieved many of his goals: to make objects exist solidly in space and form; to keep subjects from appearing to melt away because of hazy brush strokes; and to make everything in a picture seem near the surface. Here his varied blues unite all the elements, while red notes add vitality. Skillful modeling with color and deft black lines gives the vase and plate solidity. The flowers and leaves have a rich velvety texture. To create a strong geometric design, Cézanne formed verticals of the bottle, vase, and frame, and horizontals with the row of apples and the table edge.*

Cézanne *1839–1906*

CALLED THE "FATHER OF MODERN ART," Paul Cézanne belongs in the history of art next to such Old Masters as Michelangelo and Titian. Yet drawing and painting were difficult for him; he toiled, gave up, and returned to painting in a lifelong struggle. The year before his death he wondered, "Will I ever gain the goal for which I have worked so much and so long?"

A homely, shy man with a southern French accent that Parisians laughed at, Cézanne grew bitter as he lost friends, and withdrew into himself. He needed sympathy and recognition, but suffered defeat and often doubted his ability. For example, when he exhibited at age thirty-five, a critic called him "a jackass painting with his tail"; and the artist James Abbott McNeill Whistler said of a Cézanne work that "if a child had drawn it on a slate, his mother would have whipped him." Fortunately, he received financial support from his family.

Cézanne admired and studied the art of Manet, Delacroix, and others. In Paris he met the Impressionists, but rejected their emphasis on light, color, and atmosphere, as he rejected Expressionistic painters later, for he was interested primarily in *form*. He said that one must work with his eyes and mind rather than with the feelings, and study nature for solid, simple forms.

Slowly and painstakingly, Cézanne *built* a picture, fitting brush strokes in place like bricks to create solid forms and controlled space. Such painting had not been seen since the Old Masters of earlier centuries. But Cézanne created his own combinations of line, color, and structure to make new forms and spaces. He said that "painting does not consist in copying the given object mechanically; it is a question of harmonizing a number of relationships."

Objects in Cézanne's paintings were often flattened, curved objects were squared; many points of view of one form were put together to create a new perception, and planes were tilted and moved to make a new space. Whatever Cézanne painted—still lifes, fruits, mountains, rocks, people—seems to have its own *solid* structure and form. His work served as an important source for the later Cubist movement.

Only after age fifty did Cézanne win praise for his strong, rhythmic design, and for modeling with the placement of strokes of color rather than with light and shade. Shortly before his death, still struggling to find new dimensions in art, he said: "I am always studying nature and it seems to me that I am progressing slowly. . . but I have sworn to die painting."

Self-Portrait. 1879–82. *Cézanne sometimes had models sit for him more than a hundred times, as he slowly built up forms. Being his own most patient sitter, he painted over thirty self-portraits. Note how the short, parallel brush strokes add up to powerful masses. The wallpaper patterns and colors are repeated in the clothes and beard, bringing the background closer to the surface and giving the feeling that we can almost touch the back of the head and the shoulders.*

Rocks at Le Château Noir. 1895–1900. *Cézanne's watercolors have a wonderfully light, airy feeling. Here, with a few lines, he created strong yet almost abstract masses of rocks and indicated their position in space. He often left the edges unfinished in a sketch like this, thus bringing the scene into one central mass.*

Mont Sainte-Victoire Seen from Bibemus Quarry. 1885–87. *Cézanne painted this mountain again and again over a twenty-three-year period. This work is a symphony of rich colors applied with seemingly free, joyous brushwork, though we know how much Cézanne labored over each picture. Drawing carefully from nature, Cézanne shaped a more dramatic peak, and shifted spaces and shapes for a forceful design. There is a feeling of depth, yet at the same time everything is up front, thrusting out at the viewer.*

The Card Players. 1890–92. *The artist painted this particular theme five times. He portrayed the concentration of the players on their cards, creating a simple but powerful composition by joining the players through their angled arms that hold the cards. The strong vertical lines of their bodies are repeated in the chair back, table legs, and bottle of wine.*

Still Life with Apples and Oranges. 1895–1900. *A master of still-life painting, Cézanne here created a harmonious scene out of a variety of objects and shapes: fruits, pottery, and cloths. Curves, geometric designs, and bright colors move through the picture, producing a lively, rhythmic effect.*

Rouen Cathedral: Early Morning, Midday, Sunset. 1892–94. *Monet worked almost scientifically to set down dabs of color to catch the effects of light. Here are three of over twenty canvases he painted to show the facade of Rouen Cathedral as the light changed throughout the day—Monet wanted to capture each hour's color harmonies.* Early Morning *is a cool, hazy blue, before the sun has dried away the mist;* Midday *shows the bright, clear sunlight at its peak; and* Sunset *glistens in the long, deepening shadows of the evening. From close up, each picture seems a mass of confused bits of heavily applied dabs of color. From a slight distance, the patches blend together in an intense, unified image. Monet painted hour-by-hour studies of numerous subjects, including haystacks and poplar trees.*

Monet *1840–1926*

Water Lilies. About 1918. *In his last years, Monet worked whenever he could see well enough to create his masterworks—his water landscapes of swirling light and fresh color. Here he shows us water lilies on a pond, reflecting the sky. He painted this pond many times. Some of these paintings are so enormous that just one fills an exhibition room.*

CLAUDE MONET WAS ONE OF THE LEADERS of Impressionism, the artistic movement in the last half of the nineteenth century that paved the way for the free, abstract art of our own times. Like Manet, Monet sought to paint what he *saw;* yet a visual experience for Monet was not made up of form and space as such, but rather of light and color.

Thus you see a variety of colored light, which creates "impressions" of objects. If you stand very close to Monet's painting *Water Lilies*, you are not aware of outlines or edges of forms, only strokes of color; but if you stand at a certain distance you can begin to see the pond and flowers.

Monet took many years to develop his methods of painting nature as colored light. After a start as a caricaturist, in 1858 he was taken by a fellow artist to paint outdoors, and here his career really began. Artists usually made sketches or studies of nature, then in their studios they worked out the final composition; often only the original sketches retained the vitality of the scene. But, as Monet explained, he tried to work "directly from nature, striving to render my impressions in the face of the most fugitive effects."

The following year, when he was nineteen, he went to Paris to study. Soon after, he was called up for two years of military service in Algeria, then returned to

Portrait of Monet, *by Manet.* 1880. *Monet and Manet each learned from the art of the other. Although painting in different ways, for a time they worked together. A wit of the time, examining a Monet picture, said: "Monet or Manet? Monet all right, but we owe this Monet to Manet. Bravo, Monet! Thanks, Manet!"*

Paris to work. The years of struggle began. He worked hard but could not sell his paintings, was rejected by major exhibitions, broke with his family, suffered deep poverty. Once he even slashed two hundred canvases so they could not be seized by creditors. A few patrons and friends provided support whenever possible.

By 1890 he had become well known, and bought a house at Giverny. There he spent the rest of his life, devoting himself to gardening and creating his masterpieces of water lilies and nature. Unfortunately, his eyesight was badly impaired by cataracts, and his last years were marked by sadness, loneliness, and discouragement.

Gare Saint-Lazare. 1877. *Monet tackled the problem of how to paint the bluish light which floats in and out of the puffs of smoke billowing from old railroad locomotives. He was much more interested in the substance of the smoke—its color and light—than in the trains and other objects. This masterful picture is one of a series he painted of railroad station scenes.*

Women in the Garden. 1866–67. *Monet painted this poetic scene in his twenties, when he was still using figures as a major compositional element. Already, however, he was intent on the effect of sunlight filtering through trees, flowing in and out of shade, and sparkling up flowers, leaves, and costumes. He had not yet broken up form into small dabs of paint.*

Impression: Sunrise. 1872. *Monet showed this canvas in the first Impressionist exhibition of 1874. The picture was jeered at as a patchwork of color dabs. A critic said it was not even a picture but only an* impression, *thus initiating the title of this group of painters of colored light.*

Rodin *1840–1917*

"RODIN IS A TEMPEST, an explosion!" said the sculptor Jacques Lipchitz. But more often he has been called "the father of modern sculpture." Auguste Rodin departed from the tradition of his time of producing figures that were the ideal of beauty, perfectly proportioned, and without real emotions. His aim was to create human bodies that move and struggle, and to show their deepest feelings—to make them *live.* He explained that "to model shadows is to create thoughts. . . . No good sculptor can model a human figure without dwelling on the mystery of life."

Born in Paris, Rodin started to draw on scraps of paper at age nine, and began to study art at fourteen. He learned to draw and to copy paintings in oils, but his real passion was to mold things with his hands, and he spent most of his time learning to make plaster models. Somehow he failed to pass his entrance examinations for sculpture classes at the Paris School of Fine Arts, spoiling his chance of soon becoming an established sculptor. For most of his life he had to struggle to earn a living, working for a maker of plaster castings, then for decorators and public works contractors, and for a porcelain manufacturer.

He sculpted on his own time, without success. He spent almost every waking hour studying the works of Michelangelo and Greek and Roman sculptors in the museums, or working from live models, always striving to create expression and movement. He spent five years in Brussels, and went to Italy in 1875. Back in Paris, he created *The Age of Bronze,* which was accepted for an exhibition. The figure was so life-like that Rodin was accused of making casts from his live model. When photos of a real plaster cast proved the statue was original, people still disbelieved it because it looked so alive.

Though he began to receive important recognition, Rodin usually encountered severe opposition when he presented the final work. He fought with the committee of the city of Calais for ten years over his *Burghers of Calais.* The sponsoring committee for the *Monument to Balzac* refused to accept his statue, calling it unfinished. From 1880 until his death he continually worked on *The Gates of Hell,* a monumental project for the doors of the Paris School of Decorative Arts, in which he sought to express all the violence and passion of mankind.

In late years he gained many honors, and the Government gave him a studio. A year before his death, he gave the French Government his remaining works for a Rodin Museum in Paris.

Self-Portrait. 1859. *At nineteen Rodin made this sensitive drawing. He filled countless sketchbooks with figure studies, always striving to master human forms in motion. Much later the playwright George Bernard Shaw said of him: "The hand of God is his hand."*

OPPOSITE PAGE ▶

Monument to Balzac and Three Studies. 1893–98. *At fifty-one Rodin was commissioned to make a monument for the author Honoré de Balzac, who had died in 1850. He studied photos and portraits of Balzac, read his writings, went to his village, and had a suit of clothes made to his measurements—all in order to grasp the subject's personality as well as appearance. Opposite we see three examples from the more than forty studies in terra cotta, plaster, and bronze that Rodin made after a model who resembled Balzac. Gradually the final statue emerged, larger than life. The folds and curves of the robe pull our eyes upward to the rugged face. The straight line of the back of the massive body joins the oval of the sleeve and sweeping lines of the robe to form a towering, dominating bulk. When the plaster model of this work was not accepted, Rodin took it to his home and kept it for the rest of his life. This bronze cast was made only after his death.*

Rodin CONTINUED

The Thinker. 1880. *This famous statue was originally designed to sit atop* The Gates of Hell, *perhaps as a symbol of the artist as creator; a version of the statue was later used as the headstone on Rodin's grave, at his request. "What makes my* Thinker *think," he said, "is that he thinks not only with his brain, with his knitted brow, his distended nostrils and compressed lips, but with every muscle of his arms, back, and legs, with his clenched fist and gripping toes."*

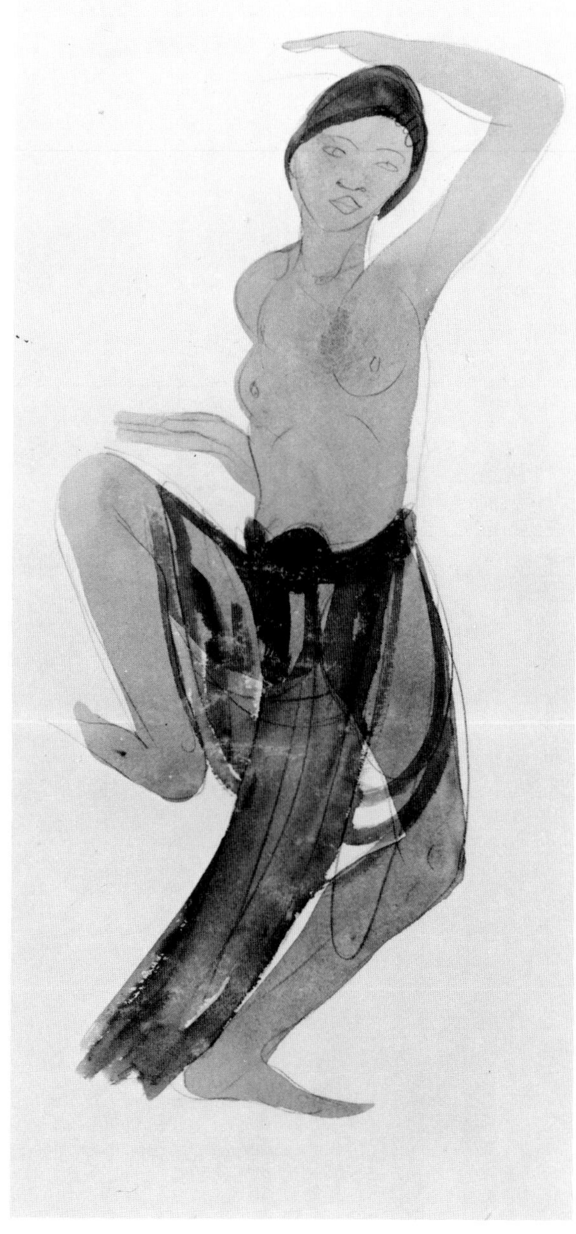

Cambodian Dancer. 1906. *Rodin made many superb drawings of figures in action, and also sketches in watercolor. He drew the outlines rapidly, usually keeping his eyes on the model rather than looking at the paper, then swiftly brushed on thin washes of watercolor, as you can see in this* Dancer.

The Burghers of Calais. 1884–86. *One of Rodin's first commissions was from the city of Calais, which wanted a figure of one of its six burghers, or citizens, who had been heroes in 1347 during the Hundred Years' War. These leaders, wearing sackcloth and ropes, gave themselves up as prisoners to make the English army stop the bloody eleven-month attack on Calais. Rodin preferred to do six lifesize figures instead of one; and rather than the expected staunch heroic figures, he created suffering men bowed in sorrowful attitudes. Though finished in 1886, the work was not installed until 1895, because of many distressing, time-consuming disagreements with the committee of Calais about the cost of casting the work in bronze, what sort of base it should have, and where it should be displayed.*

Renoir *1841–1919*

Mademoiselle Romaine Lacaux. 1864. *Renoir painted this lovely portrait when he was twenty-three; it is one of the few paintings he saved from this early period, and already shows him to be a fine colorist and designer.*

A Girl with a Watering Can. 1876. *Renoir's pleasure in young innocence glows in this depiction of a most charming subject. His skill and warmth of feeling make it a joyous expression of his love for nature and childhood. He painted this canvas at the peak of his Impressionist period, which you can see in the wonderfully loose, free dabs of paint that make up the flowers, grass, and pathway, as well as the lace on the dress and the red hair ribbon.*

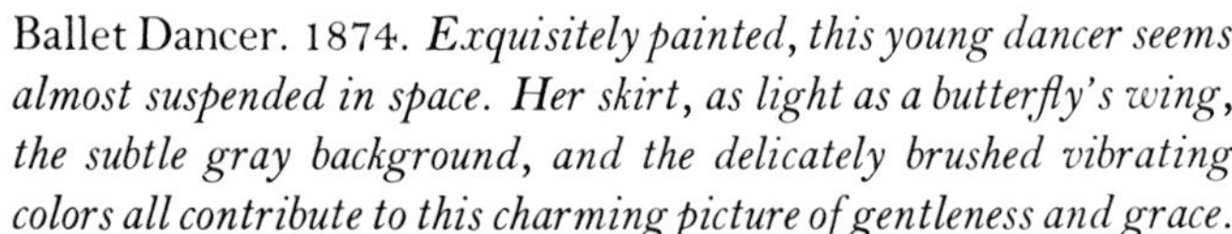

Ballet Dancer. 1874. *Exquisitely painted, this young dancer seems almost suspended in space. Her skirt, as light as a butterfly's wing, the subtle gray background, and the delicately brushed vibrating colors all contribute to this charming picture of gentleness and grace.*

ON THE DAY HE DIED AT SEVENTY-EIGHT, Renoir painted some flowers, then said, "I think I am beginning to understand something about it. . . . Today I learned something."

Pierre-Auguste Renoir is noted for the glowing color and enchantment of his work. His hand caressingly painted rounded surfaces, whether an apple, a flower petal, a bowl, or a child's cheek. He had a rare ability to capture the grace of the human body and the delicate, living colors of the skin. His interest was to portray the loves and joys of life: gay children, sunshine, trees, and above all, people. "There isn't a person, a landscape, or a subject," he wrote, "that doesn't possess at least some interest—although sometimes more or less hidden. When a painter discovers this hidden treasure, other people immediately exclaim at its beauty."

Renoir grew up in Paris, and at thirteen became an apprentice in a porcelain factory. Already determined to be an artist, he spent hours in the Louvre Museum, drawing from statues and copying the Old Masters. At twenty-one he enrolled in the School of Fine Arts, where he met Claude Monet. He remained close friends with the Impressionists, and in the 1870s his work was largely

Self-Portrait. 1910. *This sensitive picture reveals the gentle character of the aging artist. His son Jean wrote: "Renoir was discovering and rediscovering the world at every instant of his existence, with every breath of fresh air he drew." This was true even though in his last years he was ill and suffered great pain.*

Two Little Circus Girls. 1875–76. *Here you can see the influence of Japanese prints on Renoir by his placement of the figures flat against the orange ground. Note how superbly Renoir has harmonized the many tones of orange.*

Her First Evening Out. About 1880. *Here Renoir's finest brushwork catches a young girl's shy excitement at her first sight of Paris night life. To make her stand out, he painted her face and costume solidly in a large, brilliant mass of blue against a background of slashing, multi-colored strokes.*

Siesta. 1888. *This tender sketch of a girl with her dog is a fine example of Renoir's many superb drawings. Here he applied his crayon with short, rhythmic strokes. Gradually he built up the solid forms into a beautiful design of curving and vertical lines. See how he has repeated his study of the dog and the hand at the lower right.*

devoted to landscape scenes of forms bathed in light, and colors blended in gentle harmonies.

But at the same time and throughout his life, Renoir, who loved people more than the outdoors, painted portraits and interiors with more clearly defined areas of color and form. In this respect his work reflects the influences of Manet and the Old Masters Titian and Rubens. Renoir also traveled to Italy and Algeria, where the sunny colors inspired his palette. Later scenes of bathers and women were diffused with brilliant rose and orange tones.

Renoir achieved fame and financial success, but in his forties he was crippled by severe arthritis. In his last years he was unable to hold his brushes, but had them strapped to his hands, and painted furiously in spite of intense pain.

The Judgment of Paris. 1916. *Renoir was a fine sculptor as well as painter, and was inspired by the classic art of ancient Greece and Rome. In his last ten years he could not use his crippled hands for sculpting, so he would sketch his ideas, then make marks in the clay. An assistant would cut and shape the material under his constant guidance.*

Madame Tilla Durieux. 1914. *In his forties Renoir had become dissatisfied with the quick, momentary effects of Impressionism, but he always retained a loose, free brush stroke which he would combine with his "harsh" style, as in this forceful painting. For example, although the colors have become less sweet, stronger, more dramatic, and the figures more clearly outlined and solid, see how the curtain and costume sparkle with dabs of color. This design is composed of simple areas and repeated, swinging S-curves which your eyes can follow up along the arm at left, then down across the dress, and up the curtain.*

HENRI ROUSSEAU HAS BEEN CALLED A "NAIVE" or "primitive" painter. He had no formal training, but taught himself to paint. He created scenes—landscapes and still lifes—full of the freshness and directness of his untrained vision and rich imagination. Although he began working in the tradition of folk art (so-called "primitive" art), he developed highly original, enduring works.

Rousseau was born of a peasant family, and spent his childhood in the French town of Laval. He was first employed as a lawyer's clerk, then became an inspector at a toll station outside Paris. From this job came his future nickname, *Douanier* (customs official). He drew and painted all this time, but only turned to being a full-time artist after he retired from the customs office in 1885. Then he settled in Paris and the following year began to exhibit his work.

Slowly and carefully he painted still lifes, plants, and animals, which he derived from many visits to the Paris Zoo and Botanical Gardens. As a realist, he sought to show each leaf, each color. In his final work he combined these observations with his unusual imagination to produce fantastic, exotic scenes of tropical jungles and deserts, in which lush fruits, plants, and colorful animals surround strange dreamlike figures. He also painted

CONTINUED ON PAGE 126

Myself: Portrait-Landscape. 1890. *Rousseau pictured himself as a giant against the landscape of Paris, reflecting his great self-esteem. The names on the palette are of his wives. The landscape represents the Paris Exhibition of 1889: a balloon, a flag-decked ship on the River Seine, and the Eiffel Tower rising above the rooftops.*

Rousseau 1844–1910

The Sleeping Gypsy. 1897. *When Rousseau offered this painting to his home town, Laval, for very little money, it was rejected as being "childish." The whiteness of the smiling moon is reflected on the mountains, lion, gypsy, and guitar. The stripes of the gypsy's costume repeat the flow of the lion's mane, and harmonize with the shape of the guitar. These rhythms of design and color create a vast, eerie atmosphere, adding to the mystery of a most unusual scene.*

portraits of himself and his friends, and scenes of Paris full of childlike details and fanciful symbols.

Ridiculed by the public and critics, Rousseau enjoyed the support and friendship of major artists of his day —Degas, Toulouse-Lautrec, and Picasso. They recognized his importance as one who had broken away from the tradition of realism in art, and created rare beauty. Only years after he died in a hospital ward was he widely appreciated as an artist of high quality and rank.

Lotus Flowers. 1910. *Rousseau loved to paint flowers, and here he carefully drew every petal and leaf. The brilliant red and purple petals of the lotus flowers seem like the feathers of tropical birds from his marvelous jungles. The design is unified by the repeated flowers on the vase and the faint decoration on the table cover.*

The Cart of Père Juniet. 1908. *Rousseau liked to paint pictures of the people of Paris. He portrayed this neighboring family in their new cart from a photograph of the scene, but he made many changes to suit his fine sense of design. You will find the artist there, too, in a straw hat.*

The Dream. 1910. *Yadwigha was Rousseau's name for his ideal woman. He painted this vision of her lying on a couch in a tropical forest, among lush plants, birds, and animals, and the strange figure of a snake charmer. The woman is dreaming that she has been transported to a jungle, as Rousseau explained in his poem about the painting:*

Yadwigha, peacefully asleep
Enjoys a lovely dream:
She hears a kind snake charmer
Playing upon his reed.
On stream and foliage glisten
The silvery beams of the moon,
And savage serpents listen
To the gay, entrancing tune.

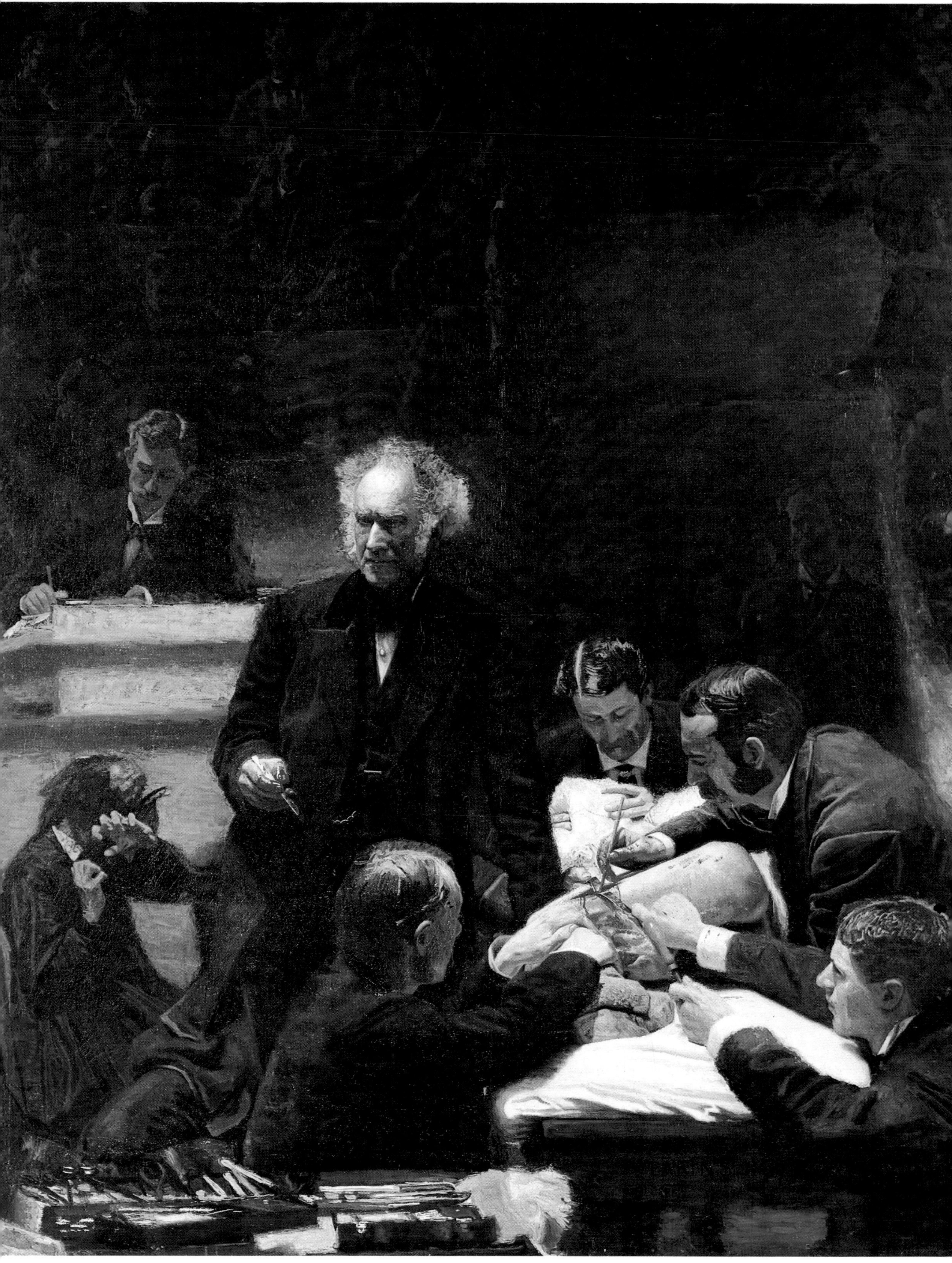

Eakins *1844–1916*

Self-Portrait. 1902. *The artist was as ruthless with himself as with others in his portraits. The intense, serious face reflects his severe character. He carefully shows his uncombed hair, the lines of his face, his wrinkled clothing, and his carelessly knotted tie.*

◀ OPPOSITE PAGE

The Gross Clinic. 1875. *The figures are life-size in this stark masterwork, one of the most powerful canvases in nineteenth-century American painting. The low-keyed color tones and dramatic lighting bring out bloody details, strongly contrasting the patient's mother, who covers her eyes in horror, with the intent scientific attitudes of the others. Eakins was called "butcher" because of this painting, some labeling it "degradation of art." Dr. Gross objected to having blood shown on his hands. Eakins never recovered from the public rejection of this monumental early work.*

THE FAMED POET WALT WHITMAN summed up his friend Thomas Eakins in these words: "Eakins is not a painter, but he is a force. . . . Tom's portraits . . . are not a remaking of life, but life . . . just as it is." Certainly one of the finest painters in American history, Eakins sought to portray reality both on the surface and under the skin. He was deeply interested in anatomy, photography, and mathematics (a science he called "so like painting"). His prime concern was to paint what he *saw* rather than to create poetic ideals. "How beautiful an old lady's skin is," he said, "all those wrinkles!" Yet his portraits were so brutally frank that sitters often did not want them.

Eakins grew up in Philadelphia. Graduating from high school at sixteen, he began his art career by studying anatomy and drawing. At twenty-two, he was one of the first Americans to go to Paris to study painting. There his teacher stressed exact, factual painting, which suited Eakins, but he refused to imitate the Old Masters. Eakins believed that an artist should paint what exists about him. Also, he had no use for the inventiveness of Impressionist art then emerging in France; he once said about a misty, poetic painting by the well-known artist Whistler: "I think it is a cowardly way to paint!"

Returning home at twenty-six, Eakins lived with his well-to-do father. He opened a studio as a portrait painter, but his work was too harshly revealing to win favor. He turned to painting sports and boating scenes, as well as faces and figures. Then, in 1875, he completed a huge canvas, *The Gross Clinic,* showing a bloody operation. Its stark realism brought angry criticism—it was too bold for its day. As Professor of Anatomy at the Pennsylvania Academy of the Fine Arts, he taught students to observe the figure inside and out. Dissecting corpses, he explained, "is hard, disagreeable work. . . . One dissects simply to increase his knowledge of how beautiful objects are put together—to the end that he may be able to imitate them. . . ." He battled Academy heads to permit the use of completely nude models, but was finally dismissed. Some of his students started the Philadelphia Art Students League, where he continued to instruct them, without pay. Eighteen years after they ejected him, the Academy awarded Eakins a Gold Medal for Excellence.

Eakins' work, portraying the middle class he knew so well, lives on for its strength and honesty. His solid, masterful paintings contributed much to American portraiture, though he was little known or appreciated in his lifetime. The great realist died in the same house where he had lived for seventy years—without causing much notice.

Walt Whitman. 1887. *Eakins' affection for his friend may be seen in this beautiful portrait, which delighted the famous poet. The artist's remarkable ability to probe depth of character and re-create the feeling of a living presence is nowhere better observed.*

The Concert Singer—Portrait of Weda Cook and Sketch. 1892. *The sketch shows us that Eakins could paint skillfully in a loose, free style. To help achieve absolute realism, he made sketches of his model each day, always in the same pose. He marked the spot for her to stand on, the point to look at. The finished portrait is unflattering in its truthfulness, but he has made the picture beautiful by painting the richly textured, elegant gown in bright light and soft shadow. Compare this portrait with that of* King Philip IV at Fraga *by Diego Velázquez. Eakins admired and studied the work of Velázquez, for Velázquez always revealed the truth in his portraits, never hiding ugliness or deformity.*

Ryder *1847–1917*

Albert Pinkham Ryder came from generations of rugged New England fishermen and grew up in New Bedford, Massachusetts, then the world's largest whaling port. The sea and the New England countryside were among his favorite subjects. He sought to portray the mystery and poetry of nature, what he *felt* as well as what he *saw*. His paintings echo the words of another famed New England lover of nature, Henry David Thoreau: "I try to see beyond the range of sight."

Ryder's education was discontinued after grammar school because of troublesome eyesight. He taught himself to paint, and made landscape scenes outdoors. In his twenties he went to New York, studied for four years at an art academy, and then made several trips to Europe. But he was not strongly influenced by other artists, and sought only to fulfill his personal visions in art. He added imaginative subjects to his landscape scenes, based on themes from Shakespeare, Romantic poetry, and opera. One of the most sensitive of American artists, Ryder freely altered the forms of the natural world to enhance these personal visions—he was truly a poet with paint.

A solitary, shaggy-haired giant with a reddish-brown beard, he had only a few friends. He never married, and cared nothing for fame or money; in later life he lived alone in a small room with his books and paints. He cared passionately about his work. He was never content, no painting was ever finished for him. He would sometimes borrow back works he had already sold, in order to "improve" them. Often, after going to sleep at night, he would rise again and again to make changes in a picture. As he worked for years on each picture, his output was relatively small—a little over 150 paintings. And, as his knowledge of painting techniques was not great, today many of his works are badly cracked.

Since his death, Ryder's work has gained much applause as appreciation grows for the expression of the imagination as well as of the eye.

Self-Portrait. About 1880. *Ryder revealed himself here as a visionary: he looked more for what went on in the depths of his mind than for what transpired in the outside world.*

◀ OPPOSITE PAGE

The Forest of Arden. 1897. *Ryder loved to read poetry and listen to opera. His inspiration for this painting was Shakespeare's play* As You Like It. *He admired and studied nature, but this landscape existed only in his imagination. The thick, rough bark of the strange tree echoes the dim figures below to the left. Soft, murky, flowing shapes convey the haunting quality of a dream.*

Moonlight Marine. 1870–90. *Ryder loved to sail on ships, and often stayed awake nights to study the quiet mood and beauty of the moonlight which haunted him. He painted such scenes over and over again, as if they were recurring dreams. It has been said of his paintings that one can feel and hear the power of the sea in them. Large, simple forms and the eerie golden light here create a lonely, mysterious mood. The many cracks in this picture appeared because Ryder paid little attention to technical needs. He used materials thoughtlessly, putting on paint and varnish in heavy layers, without waiting the necessary time for drying. Some of his paintings have cracked so badly that they are ruined; others have been saved by restoration.*

The Dead Bird. 1890–1900. *This painting on a wooden panel gives the feeling that the dead bird is already wasting away, soon to become a delicate skeleton. Even with Ryder's usual thick paint, the texture is soft, feathery, reflecting his tenderness for all things. The picture is reproduced here in its actual size.*

The Race Track. 1895–1910. *A friend of Ryder's committed suicide after losing all his savings at the race track. Filled with anger and grief, the artist painted this imaginative, dramatic picture. Death is everywhere—in the menacing serpent, the skeleton-like rider, and in the black cloud overhead, reaching out like a grasping hand.*

Tahitian Landscape. 1891. *The dramatic landscapes of South Sea islands fascinated Gauguin. He painted this sunny scene in simple flat areas of warm bright colors, colors reflecting his deep* feeling *for nature rather than colors he may have seen with his eyes. As you can see in the distant mountains, orange-red (vermilion) was one of his favorites.*

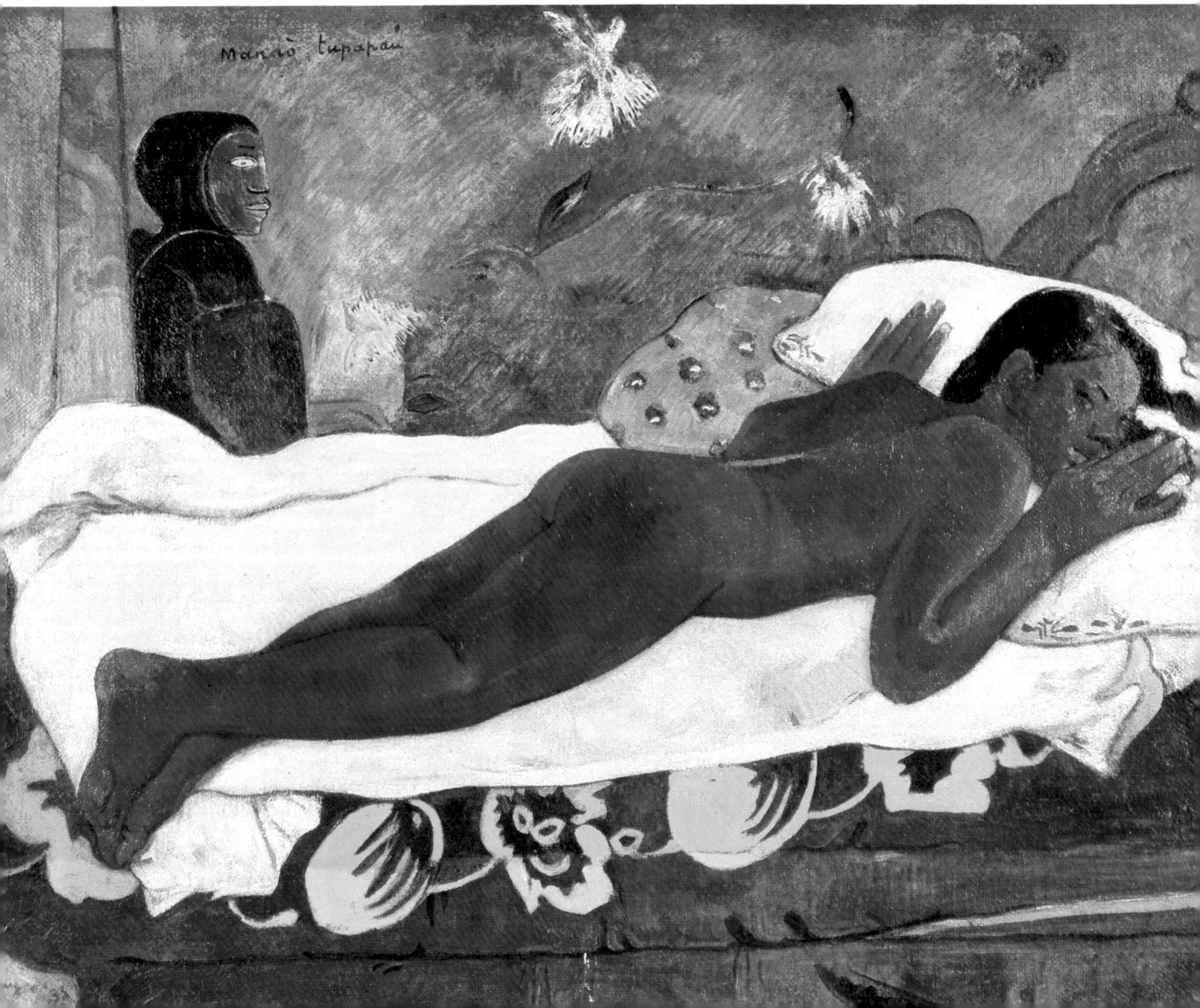

Gauguin *1848–1903*

Self-Portrait Dedicated to Vincent van Gogh *(portion).* 1888. *"I've painted a portrait of myself for Vincent," Gauguin wrote. "It is very special: total abstraction. The eyes, mouth, and nose are like flowers on a Persian carpet, thus personifying the symbolic effect." He painted on the canvas the words* les misérables *(the miserable ones)* . . . Vincent . . . Gauguin, *commemorating forever the tragic months the artists spent together in southern France, when in a rage Van Gogh cut off his ear. But Van Gogh said of Gauguin's work, "Everything he does is somehow gentle, heartbreaking, astonishing."*

◀ OPPOSITE PAGE

The Spirit of the Dead Watches. 1892. *This painting clearly shows us how beautifully Gauguin expresses the visions and passions of men's minds through symbolic objects and colors—in this case, fear. One night in Tahiti he returned to his hut to find a native girl lying on a bed, afraid of the darkness. For Tahitians the night meant that the spirits of the dead were watching, and so Gauguin depicted a spirit at his watch, as he thought the girl imagined him to look. By this time Gauguin had achieved a remarkable ability to combine solid forms of objects and flat elaborate patterns in brilliant harmonies of color.*

PAUL GAUGUIN, like his contemporary Vincent van Gogh, broke away from the current Impressionist movement in France in order to create an art that expressed the visions of his *mind* rather than of his *eye.* He developed a style in which the emphasis was on bold, simple lines and clearly defined areas of color. Unlike the Impressionists' organization of a variety of colors put on in many small strokes to create an illusion of a natural scene and space, Gauguin's colors did not attempt to reproduce reality. He freely placed large, curving areas of vivid reds, oranges, blues, and greens next to each other so that they seem to "sing" in glorious harmony. Thus line and color came to be used for expressive (and thus abstract) rather than naturalistic means. This work of Gauguin, as well as that of Van Gogh and several others, has come to be called Post-Impressionist to denote a period of transition from Impressionism to the great abstract art of the twentieth century.

Born in Paris, Gauguin spent four childhood years in Peru, then grew up in Orléans, France. At seventeen he joined the merchant marines for six years. Then for the next twelve years he worked successfully in a stockbrokerage firm, married, and settled down. During this period he began drawing and painting as an amateur, and collected Impressionist paintings; he even exhibited with the Impressionists twice. At thirty-five, there was a market crash, and Gauguin quit his job. He decided to devote his full time to painting and moved with his Danish wife and the children to Copenhagen. When an exhibition there of his work was a failure, he went back to Paris, where he lived in extreme poverty. But he did not care so long as he could paint. From then on he saw little of his family, for which he has been criticized. Years later, his son Pola wrote: "We have no reason to regret, for left to his own devices, Gauguin was able to devote himself entirely to his art. . . ."

But Gauguin was a restless man, and continued to travel. He painted in Brittany in northern France. Soon after, he sailed to the island of Martinique in the West Indies. There he became ill, and returned to Paris. Shortly he again left "the artificial world of cities" to work among French peasants. Aged forty-three, he went to Tahiti in search of an unspoiled environment. Though sick and feverish much of the time, he kept drawing, painting, carving. Several times he returned to Paris, but failing to sell his work, fled again to the South Seas. Penniless, ill, he quarreled with officials, was unjustly imprisoned, and tried to kill himself. Yet still he painted, creating some of his finest works. In May of 1903, the artist who had forsaken all family, wealth, and friends for his overwhelming passion for painting, and whose work would soon be greatly admired throughout the world, died alone in his island hut.

Noa-Noa. 1895–1900. *This watercolor is an illustration for a book Gauguin wrote about his life. The graceful nude woman in a Tahitian landscape was a favorite motif in his work; she appears in numerous drawings, watercolors, and paintings.*

Still Life with Head-Shaped Vase and Japanese Woodcut. 1889. *This bright still life almost bursts with color. The table is pink, the wall sunny yellow (colors he was to use often in his later South Sea paintings). The print on the wall again shows his interest in Japanese art. About the vase, which he had shaped himself, he said. "It represents vaguely the head of Gauguin the savage."*

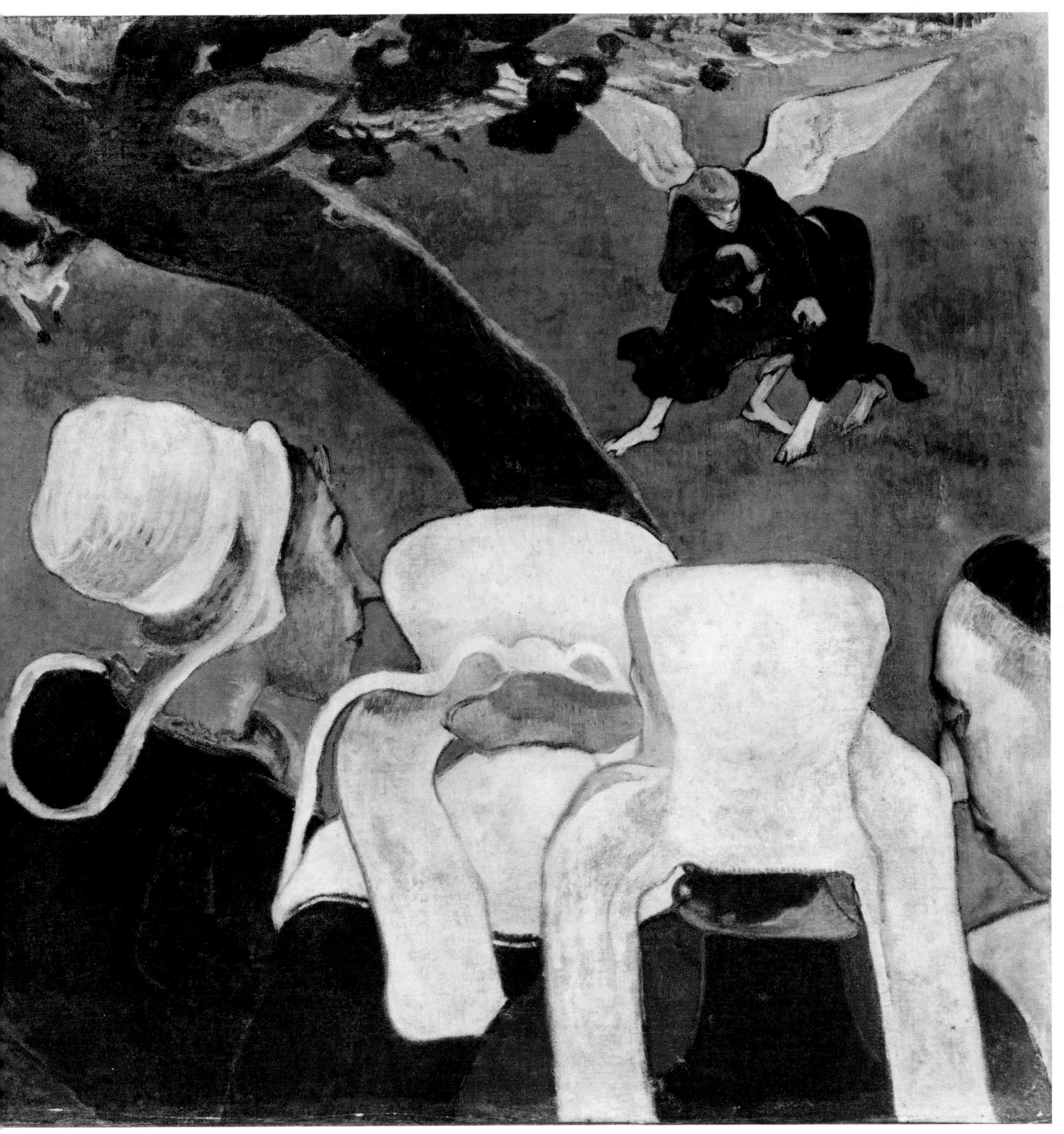

The Vision after the Sermon (Jacob Wrestling with the Angel). 1888. *Gauguin pictured a Biblical vision of the peasant women of Brittany after a church sermon. He explained: "I have attained in these figures a great rustic and superstitious simplicity. . . . There is a contrast between these real people and the struggle in a landscape which is not real and is out of proportion." The patterns formed by the diagonal tree and curving shapes are like those found in Japanese prints, which Gauguin admired. He offered the painting as a gift to a local church; the priest feared it was a practical joke and refused it, saying that his people wouldn't understand it.*

Sunflowers. 1888. *Van Gogh decorated his room in Arles with brilliant sunflower pictures. In this painting, his favorite yellow glows everywhere in thick, swirling strokes. Vincent arose early, picking flowers at full freshness to create this tribute to nature. "I still love art and life very much," he noted, shortly before his suicide.*

Van Gogh *1853–1890*

"THAT WHICH FILLS MY HEAD AND HEART must be expressed in drawings and pictures. . . . I am in a rage of work." So wrote Vincent van Gogh, one of history's most exciting artists, but a tormented man.

Born in Holland, the son of a Dutch Calvinist minister, Van Gogh failed in almost everything he tried. He grew into a homely, blue-eyed, red-haired man, who loved people yet repelled them with his inner violence. At twenty-two, burning to carry the message of God, he trained for the ministry and served as a missionary among poor Belgian miners. He suffered as they did—starving, freezing, ill—but the people turned away from him, and he was dismissed.

Heartsick, Van Gogh struggled to make his way, yet he was always rejected by other people, and felt lost and forsaken. Then, at age twenty-seven, he became obsessed with art. His early drawings were crude but strong, full of feeling: "It is a hard and difficult struggle to learn to draw well . . . I have worked like a slave. . . ."

His understanding younger brother, Theo, an art dealer, gave him support with money and love, and was the cne source of happiness in the artist's sad life. In his early thirties, Vincent visited Theo in Paris, where, inspired by Impressionist artists and their work, he discovered color. But their art was not free enough for him; he wanted to burst loose of any bonds of natural color

CONTINUED ON PAGE 143

Self-Portrait with Cut Ear. 1889. *Having met the artist Paul Gauguin in Paris, Van Gogh invited him to Arles to live and paint. A warm friendship soon ended in violent quarrels. One day Van Gogh attacked Gauguin with a razor. Later, in a frenzy, he slashed off part of his own left ear. Soon after, he painted this powerful, brooding self-portrait.*

Crows over the Wheat Field. 1890. *This is probably Van Gogh's last painting. Death seems to hover in the beating wings of the threatening black crows, whose harsh lines are repeated in violent strokes in the sky and fields. The dark sky bears down, the rutted road stops, leading nowhere. In his words: "There are vast stretches of wheat under troubled skies, and I did not need to go out of my way to express sadness and the extremity of loneliness."*

"La Mousmé." 1888. *About this sensitive, loving portrait, Van Gogh explained: "A* mousmé *is a Japanese girl—Provençal [born in Provence, France]: in this case—twelve to fourteen years old." He painted her with magnificent artistry, the curving chair repeating the lovely oval of the face, the graceful hand and the stripes of the sweater adding a gentle harmony. He admired Japanese art, saying: "The artist studies a single blade of grass. . . [which] leads him to draw every plant and then the seasons . . . [with] extreme clearness . . . as simple as buttoning your coat."*

and light, and he painted in blazing colors. Van Gogh's work helped start the later Expressionist art movement of unlimited color and emotional expression.

In 1888 Van Gogh went to Arles, a village in southern France, where he worked in a frenzy of creation—using brush, palette knife, even squeezing colors directly from the tube onto canvas. Painting frantically, he turned his seething visions into masterpieces. Still, his pictures did not sell, despite Theo's untiring efforts. Vincent suffered a series of nervous breakdowns and entered a mental hospital. Confused, deeply depressed, and lonely, but still painting furiously, he wrote: "I have tried to express the terrible passions of humanity. . . ." Only thirty-seven years old—ten short years after he had started drawing seriously—he killed himself. Theo, grief-stricken, died six months later.

Starry Night. 1889. *Although Van Gogh's work seems spontaneous, it grew out of masterly control developed from drawing and painting tirelessly. He was always trying to do better (he painted several versions of this subject). Here his short, forceful pencil strokes spiral around the moon and stars so vigorously that even in a black-and-white drawing we feel the blinding brilliance of his vision. The tall cypress trees surge upward like flames, furthering the effect of a sky on fire.*

Seurat *1859–1891*

IN HIS SHORT LIFE, until his sudden death at thirty-one, Georges Seurat created some of the most beautiful drawings and paintings in art. Called "the scientific artist," he developed a way of seeing and painting which profoundly affected the art world, especially the major painters of his day. Gauguin, Toulouse-Lautrec, Van Gogh—all worked for a time in a similar style.

Living in a middle-class area of Paris, Seurat was sketching by age seven and entered art school at fifteen. He studied with a follower of the great draftsman Ingres, and became absorbed in drawing. He soon concentrated on the science of color, reading everything he could about it. He pondered: how could various colors be placed next to each other to affect the eye and mind of the viewer, to produce the greatest intensity? He sought "a formula for optical painting. . . . I wanted to get through to something new."

By age twenty-four, he had developed this new art in his drawings. With sensitive handling of darks and lights, he simplified nature, flattening out figures and objects. After making countless drawings and oil sketches in preparation, he made a large painting of bathers. It was hung in an exhibition of the Group of Independent Artists in 1884. The dramatically different picture appealed to other artists, and as a result Seurat became a leader of a movement called Neo-Impressionism.

Instead of trying to capture a moment of nature's fleeting light, as Monet did in his paintings of Rouen Cathedral, Seurat based his work on theories of color, painting scenes with many short, even brush strokes or dots of pure colors. Because he used little points of color, his painting was called "Pointillism"; he preferred the name "Divisionism"—the dividing of space with dots of color which blended into a unified picture when viewed from a distance. What we see, unlike the depth and atmosphere in Impressionist paintings, are flat, geometric patterns. His methods were so exact that by mixing each color beforehand, he could work on a canvas by sunlight, and still paint at night by weak gaslight, knowing just what the result would be. He took over a year to complete each of his larger canvases.

Because Seurat cared mostly about color and pattern, the people in his paintings seem to have no personality, and stand fixed in stiff poses like figures in a wax museum. However, his pen and brush produced rich textures and soft surfaces that make his paintings warm and appealing. When friends praised the lyrical loveliness of his pictures, he said: "They see poetry in what I have done. No, I apply my method—and that's all there is to it."

Portrait of Seurat *by Ernest Laurent.* 1883. *Seurat was a shy, bearded, tall man. Here he is depicted by a fellow artist who worked in the same style: many thick, short lines of the crayon are drawn to produce an image barely discernible, but seeming to glow in the soft, shadowy background.*

Sunday Afternoon on the Island of La Grande Jatte. 1883–86. *This scene is considered by many to be the most important French painting of the 1880s. Seurat planned the work in every detail, according to his theories of color, making hundreds of preparatory drawings and over thirty oil sketches. Every point of color is placed with great care—nothing could be changed without destroying the harmony. The effects of vertical and horizontal "lines" against curving forms of sails, parasols, and the dog's tail form a marvelous design. The usual lively Sunday family activity has been stilled, the figures are like statues, and there is a feeling that time has stopped.*

The Steamboat. About 1886. *A friend said of Seurat: "He executed some four hundred drawings, the most beautiful painter's drawings in existence." Usually Seurat used black crayon on thick, rough paper, leaving flecks of white to create a shimmering effect. In the darkest areas he rubbed his blacks to a rich, velvety texture, contrasting strongly with his whites, such as water and smoke. Thus he created wonderful patterns of tone and simple shapes, producing a hushed, mysterious effect.*

La Parade (Invitation to the Side Show). 1889. *Seurat often pictured the entertainment world. The influence of Piero della Francesca is clear in this scene in the placement and forms of the figures. The artist's break-up of space into rectangular areas was a prophecy of art to come in the twentieth century.*

Port-en-Bessin, Entrance to the Harbor. 1888. *Seurat transformed nature's variety of shapes into elegant, quiet patterns of the ovals of cloud shadows, the delicate forms of sails, and the gentle curve of the shore. His paintings and drawings of sailboats have a special serenity, almost a total stillness.*

Toulouse-Lautrec

1864–1901

Self-Portrait *and photo. The artist turned his sharp eye on himself in swift, sharp caricatures exaggerating his misshapen body and features. Actually, he dressed well and bore himself with dignity, wearing a derby hat and often carrying a short walking-stick that he called "my button hook," which you can see in the photograph.*

HENRI DE TOULOUSE-LAUTREC has become a legendary figure in modern art. More brilliantly than any other artist of his time, perhaps, he has portrayed Paris of the 1890s—the circus, music halls, theaters, and cafés in the Montmartre section of the city. In paintings, drawings, lithographs, and posters he recorded the realities of everyday life: "I aim at rendering the true, not the ideal." But to his careful observations he added touches of beauty, such as lush fur costumes, and to his figures a certain elegance, through his graceful, flowing lines. Lautrec was a contemporary of the Impressionists, but his art stood by itself—a personal, *expressive* art combining the real and the ideal.

Lautrec's life was brief—he died of a stroke at thirty-seven—and tragic—his body was crippled when he was a young boy. He was the son of the Count of Toulouse, a wealthy French nobleman who was a sports enthusiast and largely ignored the artistic activities of his handicapped heir. When three years old, the child was asked to write his name. "I can't," he said, "but I'll draw a bull." At fourteen, Henri suffered fractures in each leg, which never healed properly and which stunted his growth. (He grew to be only four feet, six inches tall.) His mother, who would always be a great support to her son, encouraged him to paint while recovering from the accidents.

He soon decided to devote himself to a career as a painter. After a period of formal training, he left his family to live in Paris. There he developed his famous style. He haunted music halls, cabarets, and cafés in Montmartre. He also sketched at theaters, the opera,

CONTINUED ON PAGE 150

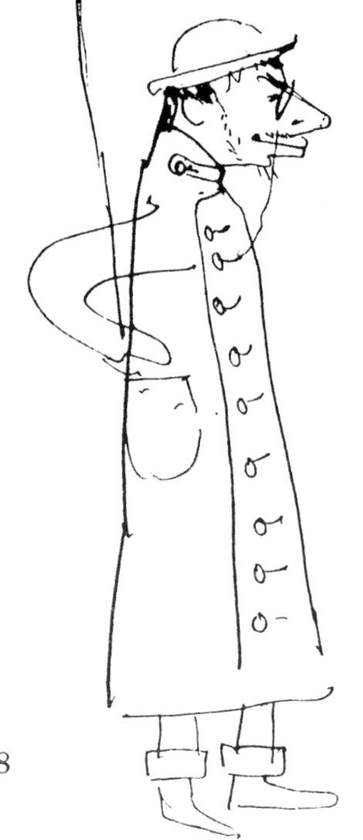

OPPOSITE PAGE ▶

Divan Japonais. 1892. *Lautrec was a master of lithography (see Glossary). He made hundreds of beautiful lithographs and thirty-one poster masterpieces from carefully planned drawings. He aimed for simplicity, using large, flat areas of bright, contrasting colors to catch the eye and convey the story quickly. He became well known as these posters were seen throughout the city, introducing Parisians to colorful new directions in this art. This poster, for a cabaret called the Divan Japonais, instantly gives us the idea of musical entertainment: the striking figures of the onlookers, the orchestral instruments and the conductor's arms, the stage, the singer. Yet we see none of these things completely—like Manet and Degas, Lautrec created "photographic" views, partly for the effect of realism, partly for an exciting design.*

Divan Japonais

75 rue des Martyrs

Ed Fournier
directeur

HTLautrec

IMP. EDW. ANCOURT, PARIS

horse races, circuses, and hospitals and law courts. Entertainers, artists, and writers accepted him for his sharp wit, his talent, and his gentlemanly courtesy to all. Thus, he was welcome to observe them at any time, and made countless drawings and even paintings on the scene that brilliantly captured the characters of the various types of people. With a few quick black lines, which seem so rich and flowing, he could give a special beauty and liveliness to the harshness of real life.

Lautrec was not bitter or self-pitying, but his life was lonely and he found it hard to bear his injuries. As one critic noted, his pictures "exhaled an inner sadness." He worked until his death, using all the graphic mediums as well as oil, pastel, gouache, painting on many kinds of paper, cardboard, and canvas. He revolutionized the art of poster painting. His work was to have a great impact on artists emerging in the early years of the twentieth century, such as Picasso and Modigliani.

In the Circus Fernando: The Ring Master. 1888. *This painting, the first of Lautrec's exciting circus pictures, shows the influence of Japanese prints. Objects are outlined simply, the curves and straight lines forming a rhythm, and many color areas are quite flat. Superb drawing brings out the dramatic action of the fierce ringmaster, the horse's plunging stride, and the agility of the rider. Typical of his bold designs, here Lautrec has chopped off figures on all sides in order to focus our eyes on the colorful center of activity.*

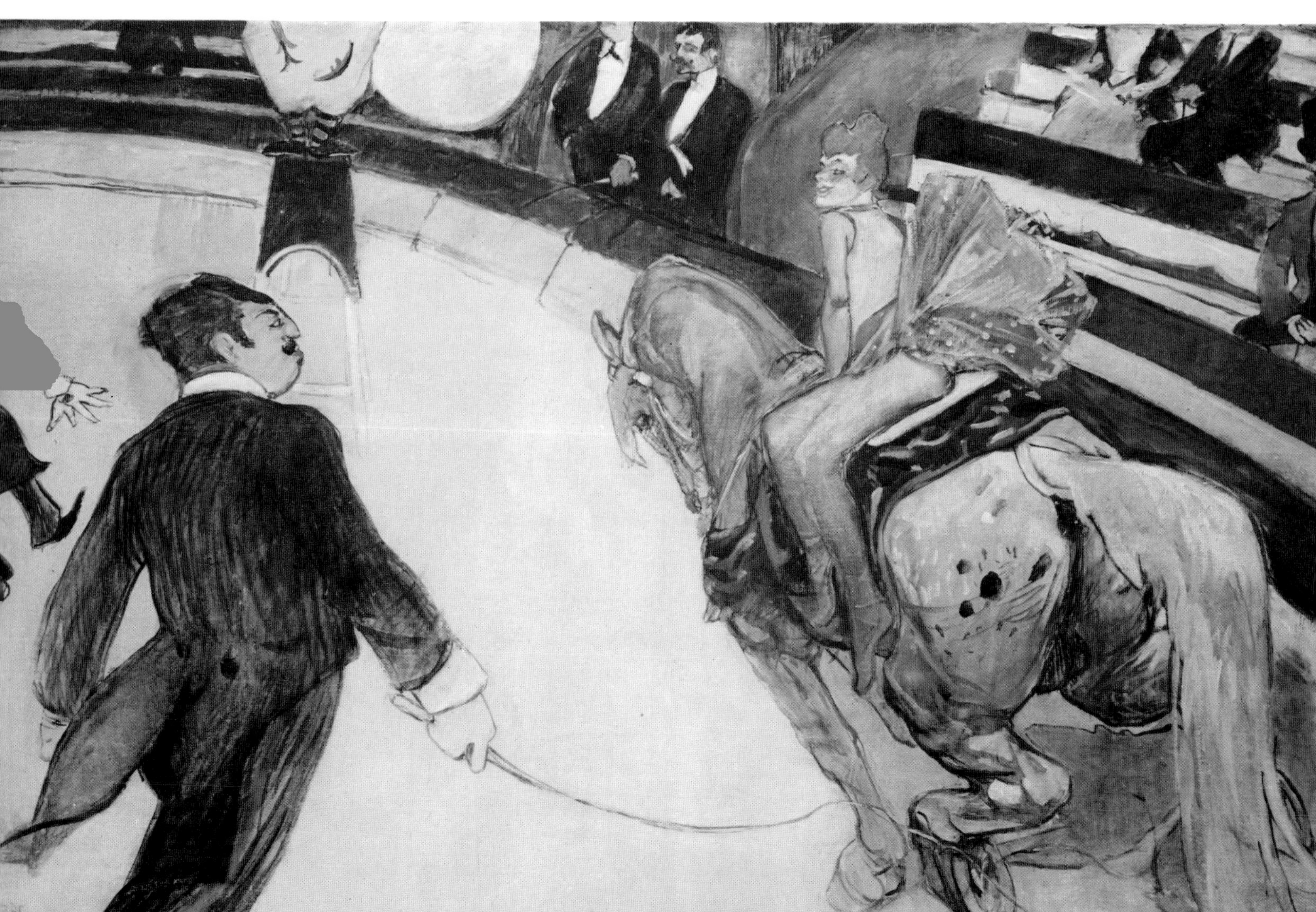

At the Moulin Rouge. 1890. *In his pictures of the famous Moulin Rouge cabaret, Lautrec often drew and painted at the same time, giving action to every figure and revealing each personality. See how the blank or grimacing face of each person here becomes a portrait. Some of Lautrec's oil paintings, like this one, have a chalky look because he painted on cardboard, which absorbs some of the color brilliance.*

Monsieur Boileau in a Café. 1893. *This is a good example of Lautrec's rare ability to bring out the character of a subject with a few expressive lines—the turn of the head or body, the tilt of a hat. The standing, white-bearded figure at the rear of this picture is the artist's father; the heavy man at the front table is a friend. Compare the zigzag of this composition to the pattern in Degas'* Absinthe *painting.*

Small Pleasures. 1913. *We can try to find some of the "real" images in this colorful painting—a mountain with churches, a sailboat, a horse, a bright pink sun. But they are merely suggested, for the picture is basically an abstract invention. The dramatic shapes circling the center mountain seem to be pushing against it, as if striving to reach the top. Kandinsky made several versions of this painting, searching for brilliant color effects. He said that colors affect the mind and soul with their vibrations. Each hue, he claimed, carries a different meaning, such as yellow—energy; white—harmony; black—silence or death; blue—depth or calmness. He noted: "vermilion [vivid orange-red] has the charm of flame, which has always attracted people."*

Kandinsky 1866–1944

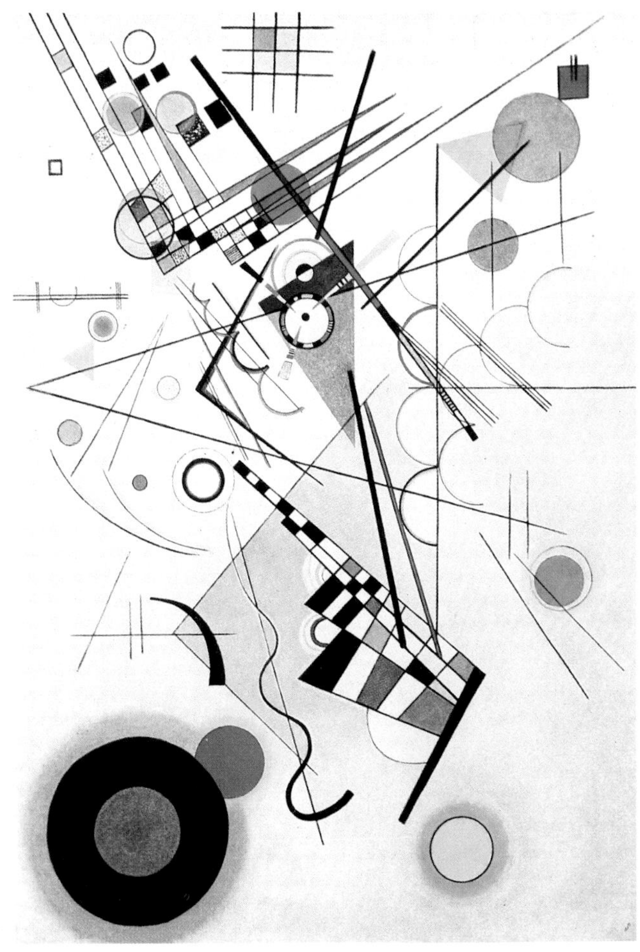

Composition VIII. 1923. *Kandinsky called this one of his finest works. He used precise, geometric shapes, stating: "I love the circle today as I formerly loved the horse. . . . I have said a great many new things about the circle. . . ." Every circle, shape, and line combines to form a powerful design; removing any one element would upset the harmony.*

WASSILY KANDINSKY AND HIS FOLLOWERS developed a new language in art. They cast off the traditions of representational art—that objects must be painted as seen by the eye—to create a new art of the abstract. Kandinsky wanted to emphasize colors and forms for their own sake. After seeing the Impressionist paintings of Monet, he wrote: "I wondered whether it would be possible to go further in this direction. . . . I had gotten 'eyes' for the abstract in art."

"Abstract" for Kandinsky, however, was not a style based on visual experiences (as with the Impressionists), or on intellectual concepts (as with Mondrian), but on the state of his emotions. His own feelings provided the inspiration for his paintings. Through symbols, shapes, lines, and colors he sought to express what he called "the spiritual in art." He developed a style that is visual "music"; when you study his work, you see vigorous rhythms of color and line, swirling in, out, and around each other. The shapes and colors, without resembling anything "real," do affect one emotionally—as you view his pictures, you may react with laughter, or feel sad, or become excited or angry.

Born and raised in Moscow, Kandinsky had little artistic training as a youth, but loved to draw, and painted in his spare time at the University, where he studied law. The warmth and the vibrant colors of his native land appear in much of his work. At thirty he went to Munich,

Bavarian Mountains with Village. 1909. *In his early period, before developing his fully abstract work, Kandinsky created a series of delightful landscapes with the flavor of Russian folk art. Colors and forms were becoming more important to him than realism. He was already blending shapes and tones, much as a composer of music combines notes into a harmonious symphony.*

Kandinsky CONTINUED

Germany, and began painting seriously. At first he painted landscapes or scenes from fairy tales; then, in 1910, he painted his first purely abstract work. The following year he formed a group called *The Blue Rider* (named after one of his pictures) with other artists seeking to paint emotional, or expressionist, themes.

He returned to Russia for a few years, then in 1922 went back to Germany, where he taught at the famous German art school, the Bauhaus. This school taught all areas of art and architecture, as well as practical crafts and industrial design. It was closed by the Nazis in 1933 and Kandinsky fled to Paris, where he became a French citizen and spent the rest of his life. His work is among the best of "Abstract Expressionist" and "Non-Objective" art (objects not recognizable), which later became major American movements and spread to other countries.

Photograph of Kandinsky in Paris, 1935.

No. 683. 1941. *Kandinsky's style of painting shifted several times during his career. In his last years, he painted abstractions of strange creatures in flat patterns. To some viewers the weird forms suggest microbes, butterflies, horses, or even snakes.*

Black Lines, No. 189. 1913. *This cheery painting with its light, floating shapes (do they suggest flowers?) sparkles with brilliant colors and crisp, playful lines. Notice how these lines contrast: some are thin and wavy, others sharp and jagged, still others heavy and dramatic. The lines create an effect of movement; they seem to move into deep space and then jump out at us.*

First Abstract Watercolor (Untitled). 1910. *This watercolor may have been the first completely abstract picture, a milestone in modern art. Like ghosts of real objects, colored shapes (which Kandinsky called "symbols of energy") rise, float, and plunge in space.*

Decorative Figure on Ornamental Background. 1927. *This unusually complex composition in flat, bright colors is an example of Matisse's rebellion against what was considered so-called "good taste" in art. He was more interested at this time in geometric structures than in natural shapes. He purposely distorted the figure to fit it into a right triangle, the vertical back and horizontal left thigh forming the straight sides. The colors are intentionally jumbled: the wild wallpaper, the patterned flower pot, the striped rug, the bowl of lemons all challenge each other. The geometric nude dominates nevertheless, as differing colors and shapes combine in total design harmony.*

Madame Matisse ("The Green Line"). 1905. *When Matisse painted this small, simple portrait of his wife, he created a daring, dramatic effect by dividing the face into separate color halves with a bright green stripe. A journalist commented, "He teaches you to see her in a strange and terrible aspect." Although the color planes of this carefully planned painting are intense throughout, the green stripe helps the head to stand out against the strong, competitive background.*

Matisse *1869–1954*

Self-Portrait. 1906. *You know that often we do not see ourselves as others see us. Matisse, a kind man with gentle eyes, painted himself with a stern gaze and mask-like face in his Fauve style of slashing black outlines and green and blue shadows.*

HENRI MATISSE HAS BEEN CALLED the greatest colorist of all time. According to Picasso, he had "a sun in his belly." Color harmonies radiating from Matisse's works reflect his love of nature's glory. He explained his approach: "I aim at an art . . . which neither troubles nor confuses. . . . I want over-tired, nervous people to enjoy a feeling of peace and relaxation when they are looking at my paintings."

Matisse studied law to please his father. At age twenty, recovering from an illness, Matisse followed a friend's suggestion that he paint to pass the time. The result was magical: "I felt uplifted into a sort of paradise in which I felt wonderfully free." While working in a law office, Matisse also went to art classes (without his parents' knowledge). Then art absorbed him totally,

The Red Studio. 1911. *When he painted this large work, Matisse was France's most famous modern artist. In typically Fauve fashion, he chose colors to suit himself, here painting floor and walls in a rich brick-red, unlike any room you ever saw. He included small copies of his own works in a fresh, gay creation of patterns of flat colors without shadows, often in the simplest outline. Matisse unified the design by placing the vertical clock in the center, like a magnet, to attract the scattered elements and hold them together.*

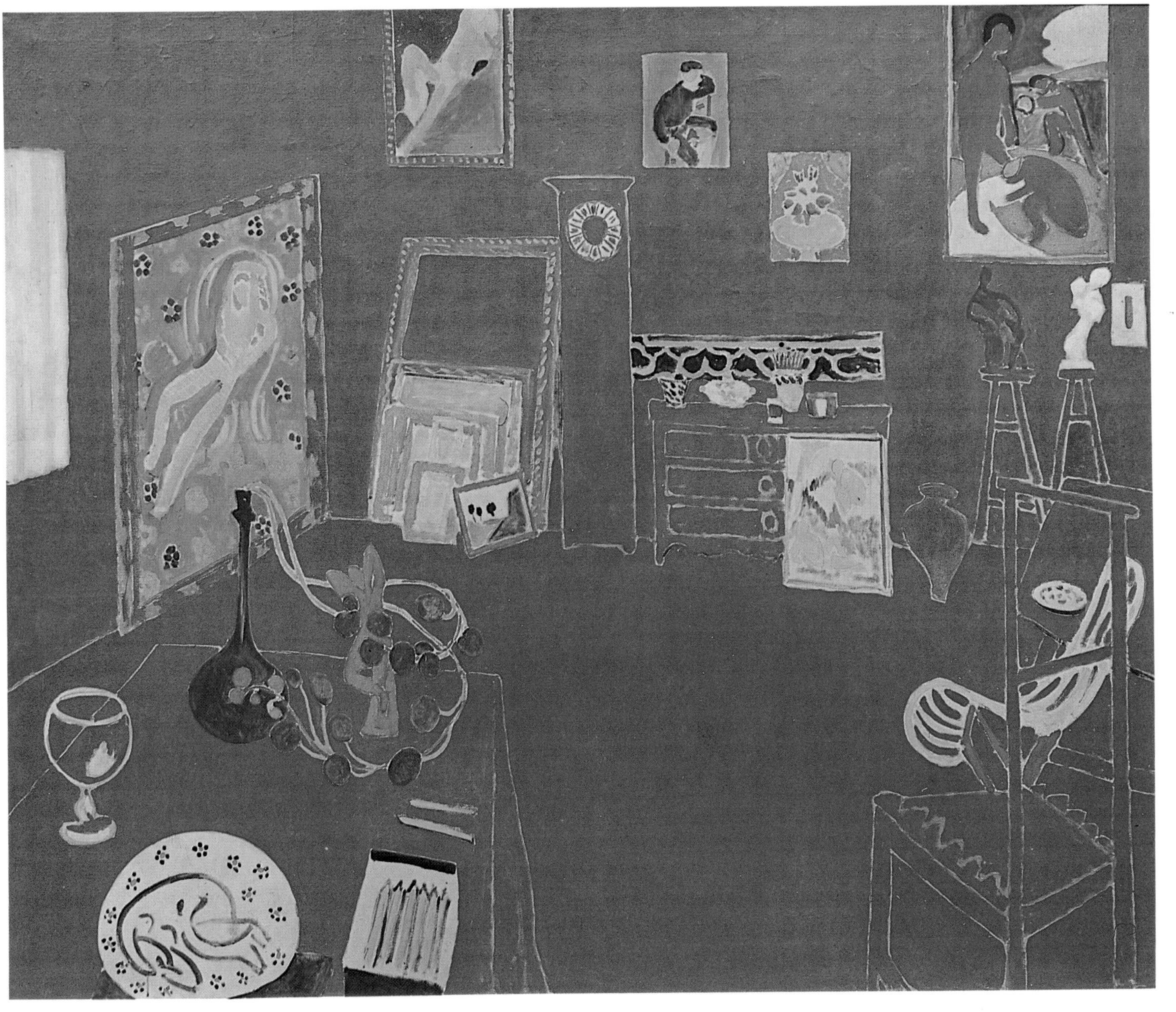

Tahitian Landscape. About 1935. *In Matisse's drawings the pen seems to dance by itself, creating lively and beautiful scenes. Matisse, a superb draftsman, achieved this effect with a few swift but delicate lines. He spent three months in Tahiti in 1930, and said that he was "fascinated, if not bowled over, by all the new sights."*

and he devoted his time to classes in which one learned by copying the masters, and to meeting other artists.

Following the dramatic Impressionists and the brilliantly colorful art of Paul Gauguin and Vincent van Gogh, another revolution burst upon the Paris art world in 1905. This was at an important annual exhibition, where works by Matisse and others were shown, dazzling in color but with little regard for nature's realism. A critic said that a classical statue exhibited among the blazing canvases was like seeing the Renaissance sculptor, Donatello, among the "*fauves*" (wild beasts).

The name Fauves stuck, and Matisse became the informal leader of the group. He developed a new style of arranging intense colors in a very personal way to keep each fresh and strong. Visits to sunny Morocco enhanced his color vision. His original patterns made thrilling music for the eye, each note full and clear. He painted his personal reaction to a subject, not a "camera" view. "Even when he [the painter] departs from nature," Matisse said, "he must do it . . . only to interpret nature better." In his mature years Matisse moved to simpler design, form, and color. His imaginative, lively sense of decoration won world-wide success. At age seventy, Matisse became ill and could no longer be very active. But in 1943 he moved to Vence in southern France, and later designed the Chapel of the Rosary of the Dominican Sisters, including architecture, decorations, furniture, and even religious garments. He completed the monumental work in four years, at the age of eighty-one. Matisse said that the whole project was "the result of my entire active life. I consider it, in spite of its imperfections, to be my masterpiece." When an expert said that "Picasso deals with love and death," another remarked: "Matisse deals with love and life."

Pineapple and Anemones. 1940. *Matisse painted some of the world's most beautiful still lifes. This one is filled with a teeming variety of patterns and colors. Note how the heavy vase, table, and fruits contrast with the lively flower and leaf patterns at the top of the canvas.*

Lady in Blue. *Early state,* February 1937. *Finished state,* April 1937. *Matisse often painted many variations before finishing a picture. At right is an early state (one of ten) of* Lady in Blue, *a free, random design. Gradually he developed the final version (below), an exciting departure from the traditional portrait. Oval shapes are repeated in graceful rhythms. Working out this "simple" canvas took Matisse over two months.*

Rouault *1871–1958*

Self-Portrait (Workman's Apprentice). 1925. *In this brooding self-portrait, Rouault pictured himself as a worker—shy, sensitive, lonely. This masterly painting may seem to have been sketched quickly, but it was carefully planned to create a strong emotional effect. The graceful black oval of the face is joined with the dark shadows of the eyes, nose, and mouth, in violent contrast to the dazzling light on the neck, cheeks, and forehead. The only colors are a luminous blue surrounding the portrait, a spot of green, and some red on the shoulders.*

PARIS IN THE EARLY YEARS of the twentieth century enjoyed the presence of some major forerunners of abstract art: Impressionists, Fauves, and Cubists. Another important movement, Expressionism, took place largely in Germany. But one Parisian artist, usually considered a Fauve, produced works of definitely Expressionist subject matter: this was Georges Rouault. Born in a Paris cellar during wartime, he remembered drawing from his earliest days, such as a picture of his grandfather's parrot he chalked on the red-tiled kitchen floor at age five.

The main theme of Rouault's paintings was his outcry against injustice. Deeply religious and moralistic, he tried to fight evil and help the poor by portraying their suffering. Filled with rage and protest, he painted ugliness and bitterness with harsh colors and bold strokes. He said he would prefer that a picture stir people's emotions rather than be a perfect painting.

Rouault's work was a radical departure from the styles of his contemporaries. As the subjects of his contempt and hatred he portrayed judges and politicians, symbols of a corrupt society. The poor, suffering victims of this society he painted as circus clowns or lonely wanderers, and he also painted beloved saints such as Joan of Arc. In his youth, Rouault was an apprentice in a stained-glass workshop. His later work strongly reflects the brilliant colors and heavy, black-lead lines of the medieval stained-glass windows that he restored. Yet Rouault's bold, vigorous black outlines and intense colors produced scenes remarkably abstract in feeling. Thus, his art bridged the old and the new.

After his apprenticeship Rouault joined an art studio, and exhibited with the Fauves in 1905. He had a successful show in 1913, and after World War I he acquired an international reputation. His late style seemed quieter, more abstract, but no less intense. Right up to his death at eighty-seven, he was never fully satisfied with his work. In 1947 he burned 315 canvases because he felt he would never have time to complete them to meet his high standards.

OPPOSITE PAGE ▶

Joan of Arc. 1951. *In this late painting, shown almost actual size, Rouault's colors were at their most glorious. Although the style seems very free and loose, the rich variations and brilliance of color come from applying layers of paint one upon another until they reach their fullest intensity. The blazing yellow sun is reflected all over the canvas, lighting up the whole picture. Rouault conveys the fervor of Joan of Arc's crusade in the bold, sweeping lines of the striding horse carrying the straight figure of the proud, armored maiden as she holds her banner high.*

The Wounded Clown. 1932. *Rouault's work never lost its depth of feeling. By showing the pain of the sagging clown and the pity of his companions, all in gay circus costumes, Rouault dramatized suffering humanity. He sometimes painted a frame on the canvas. The repetition of varying oval shapes forms a beautiful pattern.*

The Old King. 1916–38. *This is a superb example of Rouault's work. He felt that each artist should invent his own style, rather than imitate the Old Masters. He loaded his brush with almost dry paint and dragged it over other colors until it piled into rich, thick, glowing color variations. For many years he continued to add layers of paint, until he considered the picture finished in 1938. The effect, with the heavy black edges, is of luminous Gothic stained-glass windows.*

The Poor Family (Exodus). About 1911. *Rouault's angry concern for the hardships of the poor continued throughout his life. Here, under a threatening sky, a weary family rests. From the bowed-down postures of the parents, we sense tragedy and grief. The repetition of curving shapes gives unity to this lithograph.*

Mondrian *1872–1944*

PIET MONDRIAN DEVOTED HIS LIFE to his search for "true purity" in art. He wrote: "To understand, to know—there lies happiness." The painter wanted to strip art of all non-essential elements, to find a new way to express the underlying truth and beauty of nature. So he reduced his range of colors to the three primary colors (red, yellow, and blue), plus black, white, and gray; and he used only vertical and horizontal lines. His advances were so startling, yet so simple, that many have criticized him harshly. But his inventive work has affected all forms of modern art, including the design of buildings, furniture, and clothing.

Mondrian was born in Holland. He began art lessons at fourteen, then at nineteen went to Amsterdam to study. His early work was realistic. Interested in the structure of natural forms, he painted the sea, sand dunes, trees, and flowers, gradually reducing the number of lines until he achieved total abstraction.

In 1911 Mondrian went to Paris. Though influenced by the Cubist movement, he was already advancing to a more abstract style, rejecting mixed colors and curving or diagonal lines in order to make paintings of squares

Self-Portrait. 1918. *After years of working mostly with squares and rectangles (used in the background here), Mondrian painted this self-portrait in an expressive style: soft, loose brushwork in almost neutral tones of color. He was a quiet, serious man, devoted to his work and his writings.*

Composition with Red, Blue, and Yellow. 1930. *For over a decade Mondrian had been painting colored rectangles separated by short black lines, creating patterns like rows of bricks. Then he extended the broken lines to the edges of the canvas. His work became simplified, but the solid patterns of large shapes separated by strong lines offered countless variations—his work never repeats itself.*

Broadway Boogie-Woogie. 1942–43. *Mondrian spent the last years of his life in New York. He loved the flashing lights and the rhythms of boogie-woogie and jazz music. This canvas, his final painting, reflects the city's blinking signs, busy cross streets, stop-and-go traffic—the colorful patterns seen from skyscrapers. There are no black lines in this composition; instead, there are many dancing squares of pure color.*

The Red Tree. 1909–10

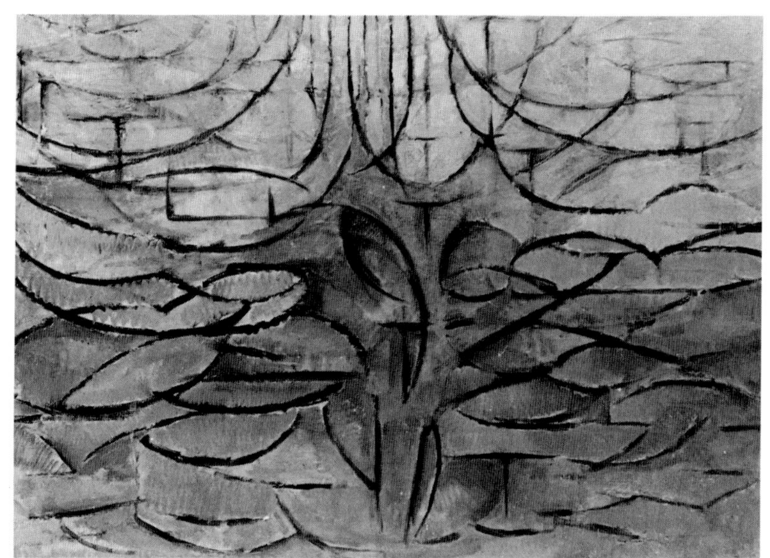

The Gray Tree. 1911

Note how Mondrian's style changed in this series of tree pictures. The earliest, the "red" tree, is graceful, realistic. A year later, 1911, the "gray" tree is recognizable, but has been broken up into a semi-abstract pattern. The next year's design of an appletree is composed of short, straight lines and slight curves, symbols *of a tree's elements rather than actual details. Mondrian moved to ever simpler patterns of shapes, lines, and areas and their relationships to each other in the canvas space.*

Flowering Appletree. 1912

and rectangles. He worked hard to achieve balance and harmony, shifting and changing shapes and lines in countless variations.

In 1917 he started a magazine called *De Stijl (Style)*, in which he published numerous essays on his art theories. He named his new art Neo-Plasticism. Yet his work did not gain popularity, and he remained very poor. Recognition came when Mondrian fled to New York during World War II. Exhibitions of his work were successful, and he sold many paintings. But he died in New York just four years later. Only after his death was his work internationally acknowledged as one of the most important developments in twentieth-century abstract art. He felt that he had found, as he put it, "a new way to express the beauty of nature . . . (to gain) pure reality."

Chrysanthemums. About 1908–10. *Three years before discovering Cubism, Mondrian painted this lovely, realistic work. At one time, against his will, he turned out many true-to-nature watercolors in order to earn enough money. Many, like this small painting, are lovely, delicate studies, capturing the natural qualities of plants, such as the variations in these petals—just one loose brush stroke establishes a form.*

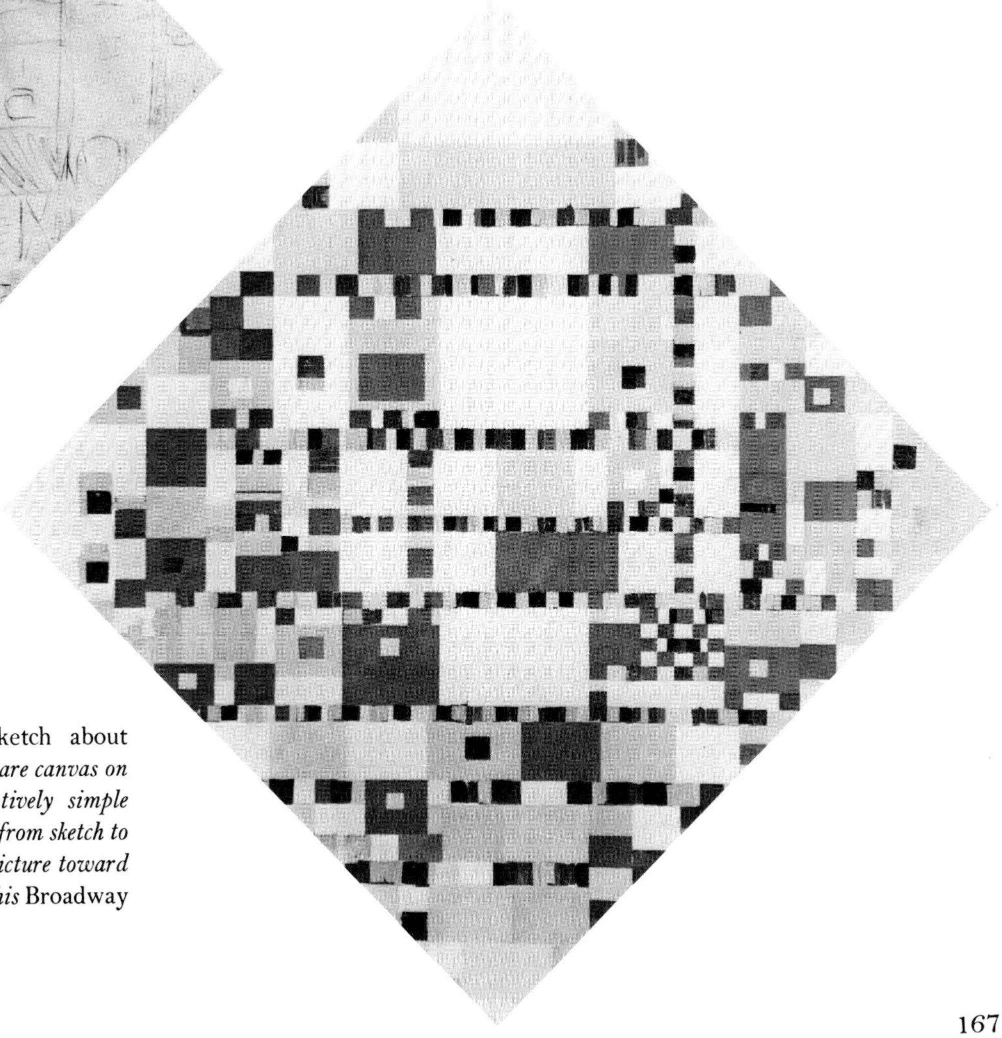

Victory Boogie-Woogie. 1943–44. Sketch about 1943. *Sometimes Mondrian turned his square canvas on end to create a diamond shape, a deceptively simple challenge. Note how the painting developed from sketch to finished work. He painted this "victory" picture toward the end of World War II. Compare it with his* Broadway Boogie-Woogie.

Klee *1879–1940*

Lost in Thought (Self-Portrait). 1919. *This drawing, made when he was forty, may not look like any photo of Klee, but it expresses how the artist felt when thinking hard about something.*

"ART DOES NOT REPRODUCE WHAT WE SEE. It makes us see," said Paul Klee, inviting us into his personal, fairy-tale world of fantasy and invention. Like a scientist making discoveries in a laboratory, Klee searched with pen and brush to find new images. He let his talent and imagination run free with colors, lines, and shapes, trying to reach to "the heart of creation."

In his work—paintings, drawings, and etchings—which he called "picture poems," Klee let his inner feelings be his guide, and often recalled images and events from his past. For example, many sketches he made as a boy contained Christmas-tree shapes, which recurred in his art years later. Images of Arabic script, square-shaped houses, the crescent moon, and tropical plants appeared in his pictures after his travels in Africa.

Klee was born in Switzerland of a Swiss mother and German father. In his teens he could draw beautiful pictures that duplicated real scenes in every detail. But he soon found that drawing things realistically was not enough for him. He began to create pictures from the "garden of his mind and heart." For a time he joined Kandinsky's group, *The Blue Rider*, which sought this kind of individual expression in art.

Klee taught art at the famed Bauhaus school (with Kandinsky) and later at the Fine Arts Academy in Düsseldorf, Germany. When the Nazis came to power, their brutality and Klee's love of freedom of expression clashed. They broke into his studio and seized his pictures, later hung in their exhibit of "degenerate art." Klee fled to Switzerland, saving whatever he could of his works. Still, he left over nine thousand pieces when he died, plus his *Diary* and many other writings.

Klee's aim was always to open up his mind and to let lines flow freely from his imagination. Like Kandinsky, he sought to show things not obvious to the eye. And his works, though designed and painted with amazing skill and insight, have a charming, child-like freshness, but were designed and painted with skill and insight that no child could have.

OPPOSITE PAGE ▶

Landscape with Yellow Birds. 1923. *Here is a beautiful example of how Klee created fairy-tale landscapes from his inner visions. Humor and mystery combine in this lighthearted watercolor. Swaying leaves repeat the shapes of the birds' yellow bodies, and clouds are like wings. In simple, colorful patterns, the artist reveals his fantasy world.*

Around the Fish. 1926. *This picture may seem child-like at first, but it was the result of the design and genius of a master artist. Klee invites your imagination to find its own meaning. Why is there a flag, a cross, and an exclamation point? Why do a line and arrow connect the fish with the man? Is that the sun and moon at the top? The answers really do not matter, as long as you seek and gain pleasure from the beautiful painting.*

Elfenau, After Nature. 1898. *At an early age Klee could draw nature beautifully, as in this sensitive drawing of a landscape near his birthplace. The original is surprisingly small, not much larger than this reproduction.*

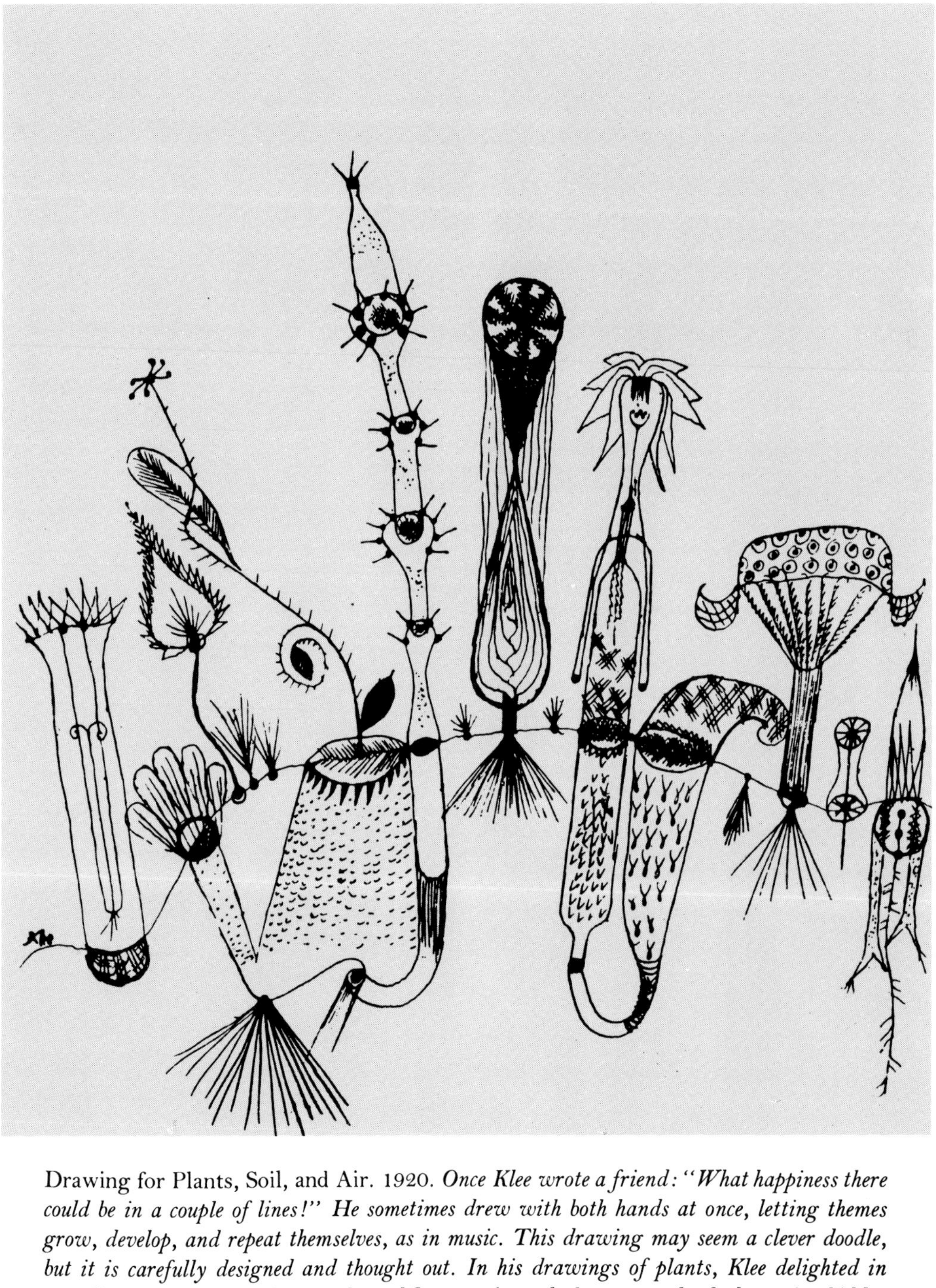

Drawing for Plants, Soil, and Air. 1920. *Once Klee wrote a friend: "What happiness there could be in a couple of lines!" He sometimes drew with both hands at once, letting themes grow, develop, and repeat themselves, as in music. This drawing may seem a clever doodle, but it is carefully designed and thought out. In his drawings of plants, Klee delighted in revealing roots, cross-sections, seeds, and flowers. As you look you may also find amusing hidden faces, hands, and figures.*

Still Life. 1940. *This powerful picture, painted in sharp colors against a black background, was one of Klee's last paintings. The oddly shaped pitcher, vases, and statue stand out against a night sky, with a full moon near the top. The drawing at the bottom left shows the angel of death wrestling with a figure, possibly a sign that Klee knew he was creating his last pictures.*

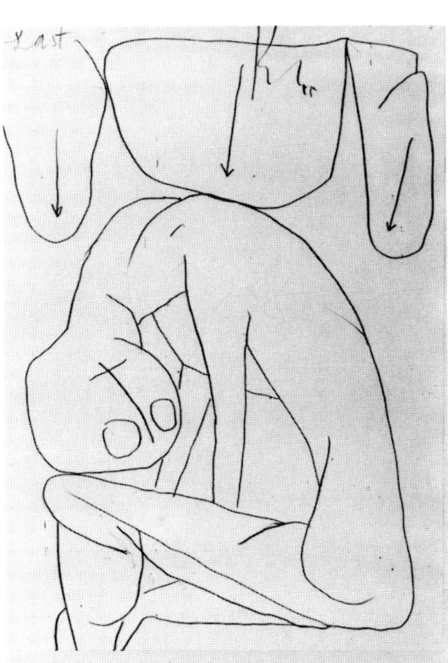

Burden. 1939. *In this simple drawing, made a year before Klee's death, arrows in the heavy, boulder-like shapes press down on the defeated figure. The frail arms can hardly support the limp body. In the skull-like head, a cross forms the nose and mouth, and empty circles make the eyes. Klee's work grew ever simpler in his last years.*

Photograph of Léger, about 1950.

Léger 1881–1955

FERNAND LÉGER was born the son of a farmer in Normandy, France. A brawny, strong-willed peasant, he grew up to become a pioneer in modern art. As other painters were attracted by figures and nature, Léger was interested in the forms of machines, which he saw as the basis of modern life. He said: "The age I live in surrounds me with manufactured objects. . . . If the whole way of painting has changed, it's because modern life has made this necessary. . . . The condensation of the modern picture, its diversity, its dislocated forms—all result from the tempo of modern life."

In Paris by age twenty, Léger started painting seriously after completing his studies in architecture. While earning his living as an architectural draftsman and photo-retoucher, he studied the Impressionists, Cézanne, and the Cubists. His style began to emerge out of Cubism and his love of the precise, geometric shapes of machinery and "the magic of light shining on metal."

At thirty, he painted *Nudes in the Forest*, in which he broke figures into faceless parts, then reassembled them to look like pipes, pistons, nuts, and bolts. The painting was well received, and was followed a year later by a one-man show. He continued to create solid, machine-like forms of flat, pure colors and dark outlines. He applied his personal viewpoint to many other fields: film, sculpture, ceramics, ballet design, stained-glass windows, murals, teaching, and writing.

After World War I, cannons and war machines appeared in his works. He kept changing his style; he would paint abstract forms, then return to realistic figures. From 1940 to 1945 he lived in New York. He summed up the fast-paced city in these words: "Bad taste, strong colors—it is all here for the painter to organize and get the full use of its power." Léger spent the rest of his long, productive life in France.

Through the years his work became more solid, seemingly purer in color and form. Always optimistic, he enlivened his subject matter with figures of jugglers, musicians, acrobats, bicycle riders, and families; he said that "beauty is everywhere, in the arrangement of your pots and pans on the white kitchen wall. . . ."

The Great Parade. 1954. *Léger was seventy-three when he painted this important work. With strong, solid black lines and bright colors, he created a composition of circus figures and machinery against large, abstract color shapes—a complicated but unified design. See how the color areas seem to go back and forth, giving the effect of lively motion. Léger said about the red circle, symbol of the circus: "Nothing is as round as the circus. . . . The ring dominates, swallows up everything. . . ."*

Three Women (Le Grand Déjeuner). 1921. *This complex masterpiece features three semi-realistic but machine-like female figures at breakfast. Their hair is like curved iron, their hard-edged limbs like polished steel, and their expressions as blank as robots'. Léger said: "The human body has no more importance than keys or bicycles." Thus, although we can easily distinguish the women, as well as the breakfast table, the couch and pillows, the rugs and the black cat at the far right, no one of these things stands out more than the others. Instead, all these elements combine into a harmonious unity of multi-colored patterns. It is interesting to compare this painting with Picasso's* The Three Musicians, *another picture full of patterns, based on Cubism, and with a similar mysterious, slightly mocking air.*

The Staircase. 1913. *Here Léger created depth by piling or stacking forms one in front of another. He formed bodies out of cones and cylinders, and drew lines with vigor to create a staircase which we see in sections in many areas of the scene. "White light" glows next to the thick lines and gay colors, adding to the rhythmic action of the whole picture.*

The Card Players. 1917. *This is one of Léger's famous "tubular paintings," made in the period when he achieved maturity as an artist, during World War I. We can almost hear the robot-like figures clanging against each other. The artist's concept of modern life—people looking, walking, and acting like machines—was strongly affected by the war. Fascinated by cannons and other war machines, Léger said: "Once I got my teeth in that kind of reality, I never let go of objects again. . . . I wished to give the human figure the same quality."*

Picasso *Born 1881*

Pablo Picasso was born in Spain but has spent most of his adult life in France. He has become more famous in his lifetime than almost any other artist in history. His adventurous genius led him to explore many areas of art: painting, drawing, sculpture, printmaking, ceramics, and ballet and theater design. His work, ranging from sweetly tender to terribly violent themes, is full of wonderful surprises. It is amazing how many styles he developed, for any one of his styles could be the lifework of a single artist.

Picasso has often made use of classical, primitive, and other art forms, which he transforms and integrates into his own work. He can paint in a clear, lyrical style, but repeatedly during his long life he has chosen to invent new forms and new interpretations of the possibilities of visual space within the flatness of a painting or a drawing. He avoids pure abstract painting; he believes that all art should start with a subject, so that a feeling of it remains no matter how it has been changed. "I treat paintings as I treat objects," he said. "If a window in a picture looks wrong, I close it and draw the curtains, just as I do in my room. . . . I want the work to reflect only feeling."

A child prodigy, he was given excellent art instruction by his father, an art teacher and painter. Young Picasso painted well by the age of ten, and was a master of drawing by twelve. At fourteen he went to Barcelona to the Academy of Fine Arts, and completed the entrance tests in one day instead of the month that was usually necessary. Two years later, some of his paintings were exhibited in Barcelona. He settled in Paris in his twenties, but continued to visit his beloved homeland until the Spanish Civil War. In Paris he developed the style known as Cubism with a fellow painter, Georges Braque. He also invented the *collage*, and created sculpture out of countless materials (from tiny pebbles or matchbooks to bronze for huge statues). The wide range of his talents and his vigorous inventive spirit place him as a great innovator in modern art, comparable to Giotto in the Middle Ages and Michelangelo in the Renaissance.

Self-Portrait. 1906. *Here Picasso gives us an expressive self-portrait—a serious, intense young Spaniard with black, piercing eyes.*

Woman with a Fan. 1905. *Picasso's paintings of the years 1901–4 make up his "Blue Period," so called because he used cold, gloomy tones of blue and chose for his subjects lonely, tragic people. In 1904 he began to lighten his palette, and introduced pink colors, as we see here. The works of 1904–6 are thus called his "Rose Period."*

Les Demoiselles d'Avignon (The Young Women of Avignon). 1906–7. *Inspired by the work of Cézanne, Picasso carried experimentation with form even further in this painting, which marks a revolutionary breakthrough in art and points the way to Cubism. For Picasso has broken up forms and redefined them in large, firmly outlined planes of color,* without *light or shadow. Yet the figures appear to be more like sculpture—heavy, solid masses. The mask-like faces were inspired by the primitive sculpture of Africa, which had lately begun to be discovered and admired.*

The Three Musicians. 1921. *Picasso soon went on to other styles. Here he painted simplified Cubist forms so that they appear to be a paste-up, or* collage—*in other words, he arranged overlapping geometric shapes that look like cut-out forms, making gay patterns of sheet music, instruments, three musicians in costumes and masks, and a dog under a table.*

The Dream. 1932. *In a calm, happy period, Picasso designed this picture of a graceful, curving beauty in joyous colors. He drew the portrait of a woman he loved, in profile and in full face, thus showing us two viewpoints at the same time—this idea was first developed in his Cubist paintings to show us more about the subject than our eyes normally see. Cover the top of the face, and you can see her profile.*

Bullfight. 1957. *Picasso often pictured the colorful excitement of bullfights. He made many quick drawings, such as this one, filled with flashing movements of men and animals.*

Baboon and Young. 1951. *Picasso often makes delightful jokes in his work. In this sculpture of motherhood—a baboon holding her baby—he created the head with a toy auto. In some other works, he made a bull's head out of a bicycle seat and handlebars, and painted a woman with a fish for a hat.*

Portrait of Daniel-Henry Kahnweiler. 1910. *From 1907 to 1915, Picasso and Braque led the Cubist movement (see biography of Braque). Compare this portrait of Picasso's art dealer and friend with Braque's* Still Life with Violin and Pitcher *to see how the forms are broken up and rearranged. Note, too, how quickly and how far Picasso has come in the development of this totally new pictorial style—just three years after* Les Demoiselles d'Avignon.

Guernica. 1937. *This masterpiece is one of the strongest protests of all time against the horrors of war. After German bombers destroyed the defenseless Spanish city of Guernica, Picasso painted this scene to show his heartbreak and rage, and to be a memorial to the city. He distorted forms, using only stark black, white, and gray tones on a huge canvas to cry out against cruel destruction. In this design of strong curves, jagged lines, and sharp angles, you will find some very moving figures: a mother clutching her dead baby, a man gripping a knife, a victim being consumed by flames, and people and animals alike screaming in agony and terror.*

Braque *1882–1963*

GEORGES BRAQUE BEGAN AS A HOUSE PAINTER and became a world-famous artist. He was born in France, almost with a brush in his hand, as both his father and grandfather were house painters and amateur artists. They taught him early the value of good craftsmanship and patient, hard work. On jobs, he painted imitation marble and wood grain on surfaces, and also did lettering. These influences showed up in his art.

Outwardly Braque was quiet, calm, and controlled. He rarely showed emotion, preferring to keep his feelings to himself. Pablo Picasso summed up this man and his art in these words: "Braque never sings off-key." Braque studied hard, and was particularly fascinated by African, Egyptian, and ancient Greek art. He joined the Fauves, the group of artists whose keynote was a wild abandon with color, but broke away after two years.

A big change came at age twenty-seven, when Braque and Picasso, influenced partly by Paul Cézanne's work, decided to paint "not what you see but what you know is there," as Picasso put it. They considered a picture no longer a space in which to depict something in a realistic manner, but something to be built by the artist. Slowly, carefully, with much revision, Braque created paintings that seemed to show only fragments of an object; yet on close examination we see how he has actually represented *all* of an object—as we would see it from above, below, and behind. This was the beginning of Cubism.

During World War I Braque entered the army, thus ending his working relationship with Picasso. He suffered a severe head wound, lost his sight for a time, and finally recovered. He returned to art more seriously than ever, and worked only to please himself, not to exhibit or sell pictures. For years he became a studio shut-in, working steadily, using odd materials, and always inventing. "Real discoveries," he noted, "are made beyond the limits of knowledge." Until his death at eighty-one, he continually created a wide variety of patterns of pleasing forms and harmonious colors, and experimented with sculpture and jewelry as well.

Portrait of Georges Braque *by Picasso.* 1909. *Picasso and Braque worked very closely together at this time. We may see the similarities in their styles by comparing this* Portrait of Braque *by Picasso with Braque's* Still Life with Violin and Pitcher. *As with the still-life objects, we can see the head easily against the background, although the face has been broken up into geometric shapes.*

◀ OPPOSITE PAGE

The Round Table. 1929. *Braque's style changed after the war. He added more color and richness to his work, and combined familiar articles such as shown here—a table, fruit, a knife, sheets of paper—to create still-life masterworks. He shifted objects about, divided them into dark and light segments, and separated and joined them with strong outlines.*

Braque CONTINUED

The Bird and Its Nest. 1955. *In his seventies, trying for new "inventions," Braque created handsome sculptural reliefs in painted plaster, and pictures of flowers and wonderful birds such as this one, a design of poetic simplicity in heavily textured paints. Braque said that his birds were not like any natural creatures but "were born on the canvas."*

Head of a Horse. 1946. *This is one of Braque's highly imaginative sculptures, in which he masterfully joined loose, sweeping forms to create a horse's head with a flame-like mane. He first made a plaster cast of the head in 1941–42. This bronze version was made from the cast in 1946.*

Musical Forms (Guitar and Clarinet). 1918. *Braque used stenciled letters, musical notes, and new textures made with substances such as sand, tobacco, and ashes mixed into the paints. To create a dramatic design of shapes, spaces, and textures, he also pasted pieces of patterned wallpaper, colored papers, and cardboard to the canvas. The name for this kind of art is* collage, *the French word for pasting.*

Still Life with Violin and Pitcher. 1909–10. *In this Cubist painting, a violin and jug are cut up like facets of a diamond in order to show various viewpoints at once. In this way the Cubists tried to put into a picture what the mind knows exists but cannot be seen directly by the eye. Braque twisted the scroll-top of the violin, and mixed flat areas and cube forms so that they seem to move into and out of the picture. He created a kind of space in motion, different from older forms of art in which we see the object straight in front of us. The realistically painted nail at the top was intended to fool the observer.*

Modigliani 1884–1920

Amedeo Modigliani said that all he wanted was "a brief life, but an intense one." This came to pass, for the handsome Italian Jew died at thirty-five, after more than twenty years of illness, poverty, and frustration. Yet his paintings of women are poems of serene beauty, his portraits are sympathetic character studies. His friend the sculptor Jacques Lipchitz said: "He could never forget his interest in people, and he painted them, so to say, with abandon, urged on by the intensity of his feelings and vision."

The only subjects which really interested Modigliani were the human face and figure. On canvas, he created exceptionally lovely harmonies of ovals, curves, and elongated forms, with large areas of rich, warm colors and delicate skin tones. His very personal style was blended from many influences: the Renaissance art of Botticelli, the Fauve paintings of Matisse, and primitive masks and carvings from Africa.

Modigliani studied art in his teens, then at twenty-two he left his native Italy for Paris. He plunged into the free, exciting Parisian art world, a center for struggling painters, sculptors, poets, and writers. He painted in a frenzy, and shared his passions and ideas with other young intellectuals. But success evaded him, and intense poverty was added to the burdens of his frustrations and violent emotions. Deeply depressed, he sought relief in alcohol and drugs, abusing his body which had already been weakened by tuberculosis and various childhood diseases. At twenty-five, he revisited Italy and showed his sculptures. Receiving severe criticism, he became enraged and threw all the pieces into a canal, where today they still lie buried in the mud.

He returned to Paris; there, people who recognized and admired Modigliani's talent could not pay much for his work. But he struggled on until his death in the Charity Hospital, just fourteen years after he had come to Paris to make a great career. His brother wired from Rome, "Bury him like a prince." His wife, Jeanne, broken-hearted, took her life the next day. Modigliani's art remains as enduring evidence of his unique poetic vision.

Self-Portrait. 1919. *The elegant forms here have the grace of a Botticelli masterpiece. Modigliani's color patterns in each portrait may seem the same at first, but differ according to the personality of the sitter.*

◀ OPPOSITE PAGE

Portrait of Jeanne Hébuterne. 1919. *Many experts consider this tender portrait to be one of Modigliani's finest works. It is a song of love for his devoted Jeanne, and may have been his last painting. Such graceful distortions are found in many of the artist's most beautiful portraits. Note the characteristics of his famous style: the lengthened nose, small almond-shaped eyes without pupils, simple, long, oval face, swan-like neck, and gentle curves.*

Modigliani

CONTINUED

Bride and Groom. 1915–16. *In all his portraits, Modigliani changed the shapes of people, outlining forms in curves and angles. In this double portrait of the well-known sculptor Jacques Lipchitz and his wife, the artist used a simple, flat design. Black lines make the patterns seem to break apart, yet flow together.*

Head of a Woman *(left)*. About 1910. Lola de Valence *(right)*. 1916. *Modigliani's pictures have been called "sculptured paintings." He was also intensely interested in sculpture, and worked in this medium whenever possible. Here is a clear comparison in the features and forms of a limestone sculpture and an oil painting. Both are strongly designed along the lines of an African mask.*

The Little Peasant *(above)*. 1918. Little Girl in Blue *(left)*. 1918. *Though most of his portraits are of grown-ups, Modigliani was fond of children and painted them with a special gentleness. These two lovely portraits show the boy and girl facing straight forward, posing in a shy manner for their artist friend. The shapes and colors are simple and flat. The faces, wearing the same quiet expressions that Modigliani portrayed in older people, are really almost abstract patterns of graceful ovals, with the beautifully drawn arches of the noses and eyes that distinguish his work.*

Chagall *Born 1887*

Self-Portrait with Seven Fingers. 1912. *Here we see the artist as he pauses in his work, dreaming of the Russian village of his childhood (his thoughts are represented in a circle of clouds at upper right), which he is trying to re-create on canvas. At left we see another of his favorite scenes, Paris with its Eiffel Tower. At this time his work shows the influence of Cubism in the use of geometric forms. A triangle forms the nose, a square makes the cheek, and a sharply pointed oval becomes a large eye. He even painted one hand with seven fingers to create an amusing effect in this exciting design.*

MARC CHAGALL STARTED LIFE in the small, picturesque village of Vitebsk in Russia. Though he lived at times in Germany and the United States, and settled in France, many of his paintings are filled with things he remembered from his "sad and joyful" birthplace. His appealing pictures are like dreams about the people, houses, and animals of his childhood. They reflect Chagall's love for his parents, eight sisters, and a brother, a very devout Jewish family. Revealing his own deep religious feelings, he said about one of his etchings: "It must sing, it must cry—it is The Bible."

A joyous man, gifted with a lively imagination, Chagall has the courage to paint his gay, fanciful visions, and the talent to re-create them for us beautifully. His brilliantly colored pictures appeal especially to young people, and those young at heart at any age. He may paint a rooster three times as large as a man, take off a person's head and float it somewhere else in the design, or draw a chicken complete with the unlaid egg visible inside it. Chagall does all this to improve the pattern on his canvas, filling empty spaces, changing, rearranging, adding to the dream-like quality and total beauty of each work. He once explained: "I upset in order to find another reality."

He applied his talent in many other directions besides painting. He illustrated books, created pottery and ceramics, designed costumes and scenery, and painted murals for theater, opera, and ballet. His marvelous stained-glass windows for a synagogue in Jerusalem are world-famous.

In all of Chagall's work, pure brilliant color charms the eye. Even his black-and-white drawings and etchings have a feeling of color in their moving lines and forms. He said: "Color is everything, color is vibration like music. . . . An artist has a born-color that is in him . . . his own color-love."

OPPOSITE PAGE

I and the Village. 1911. *This is a fine example of Chagall's colorful, poetic paintings. He places objects freely to please his sense of design, and to create a rich pattern of circles and triangles. The cow and the green-faced young man stare at each other, their eyes joined by a thin line. Part of the cow's head is blue sky, and on its face is placed a scene of a girl milking the cow. Topsy-turvy houses form the village on a snowy hill. A woman floats upside down, and the head of another figure almost fills the church. Dazzling flowers held by the man light up the picture like a sparkler.*

Chagall.
1911 Paris

Bride with Blue Horse. 1950. *Both the rooster and the bride have appeared in many of Chagall's imaginative paintings. Here the rooster seems to be singing a happy song to the bride, who wears a flowing veil and is seen both full face and in profile. The blue horse in the space at the top completes this pleasing circular design. Each viewer may find a different meaning in this delightful picture.*

The Green Violinist. 1918. *Chagall's Uncle Neuch had a beard and played the violin. Once young Chagall saw him sitting on a rooftop, chewing carrots and enjoying the view. As with other childhood memories, Chagall put a violinist in many later paintings; here he gave him a green face. The little man flying through the air at the top, another man at the left waving a violin above the dog, who is as big as a house, and the angled ladder at lower right all add to the oval design.*

The Birthday. 1915. *Remembering when his beloved wife, Bella, brought him flowers on his twenty-eighth birthday, Chagall painted this romantic canvas. He shows his feeling: "I'm so happy, I'm floating on air." The artist also twisted his neck in an impossible curve in order to complete the graceful oval design for the center of the picture.*

Women and Birds in Front of the Sun. 1942. *In spite of the title, the first thing we may notice in this lively painting is the brilliant white moon; the sun is a small but intense red ball, and there are stars of white, blue, and yellow. There seem to be two women, and a variety of little creatures—the "birds." Miró painted this scene over and over again, constantly changing the shapes of the objects and figures. But these forms, however abstract they may seem, never lose their quality of being alive, of moving about in all directions. With them Miró built up a large vocabulary of "organic" symbols, which he used throughout his career.*

Miró *Born 1893*

L'Hirondelle d'Amour. 1934. L'Hirondelle *is the swallow which flies in graceful glides. This painting is certainly an enchanting "flight of fancy," for Miró sets flying his special, imaginative creatures: birds, fish, figures, even a black cat. He uses forms freely, without trying to be realistic; an arm becomes a leg, and a leg ends in a hand. All the elements are joined by the flowing letters of the title, and the whole scene seems to swirl against the beautifully brushed blue background.*

JOAN MIRÓ'S WORK reveals all the charm, spirit, and humor of one of the most inventive geniuses in art. Unhampered by rules or styles, his work always remains free and lively, and delightfully imaginative.

Miró was born near Barcelona. He entered art school at fourteen, and his understanding teachers quickly realized that the youngster was amazingly gifted. They encouraged him to let his sense of color and his ability for imaginative drawing run free. At twenty-five, his first one-man exhibit of more than sixty paintings and many drawings was a huge success. In 1919, he went to Paris to live and work. There he was affected by the art of Picasso, Rousseau, Van Gogh, and Matisse. As his talents became known, his work was acclaimed, unlike so many artists who are unrecognized and even condemned during their lifetimes.

He returned to Spain in 1939. His painting had always been influenced by the color and life of his native land. During the Spanish Civil War, his pictures were composed of tragic shapes, with somber brown and black tones, reflecting his grief over the suffering of many of his people.

Miró said that his art was often inspired "by the material I'm working with. . . . Even a few casual swipes of my brush in cleaning it may suggest the beginning of a picture." Once, when some blackberry jam was spilled, he was so taken by its shape and color that he started a

CONTINUED ON PAGE 195

Self-Portrait. 1937–38. *As with much of his work, Miró worked over this haunting canvas for a long period. Using oil, crayon, and pencil, he created a revealing portrait alive with fanciful symbols. Pinwheels, sunbursts, starfish, stars, and strange objects move in and upon and around the face and figure. Some viewers have thought that the artist was painting an impression of himself rising to heaven.*

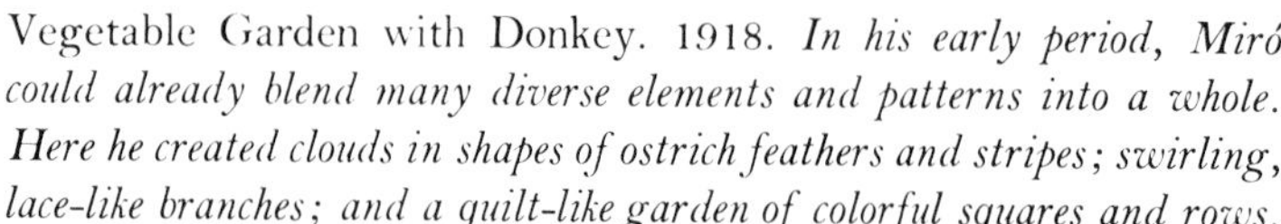

Vegetable Garden with Donkey. 1918. *In his early period, Miró could already blend many diverse elements and patterns into a whole. Here he created clouds in shapes of ostrich feathers and stripes; swirling, lace-like branches; and a quilt-like garden of colorful squares and rows.*

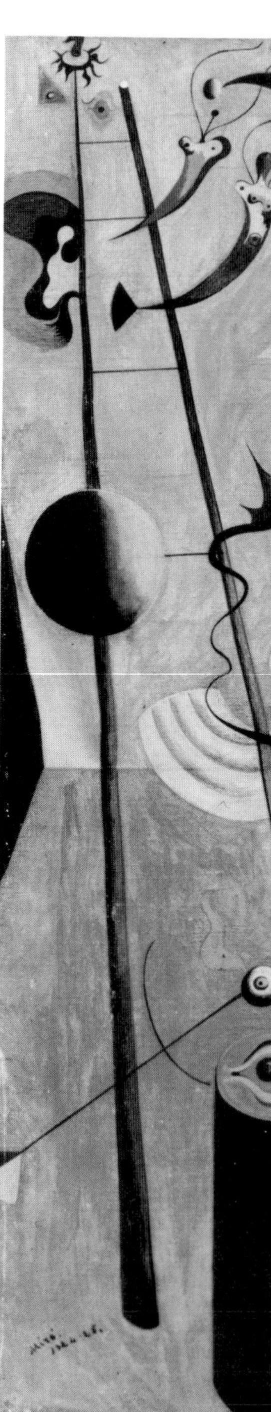

painting from it. But he emphasized that from such free beginnings his work grew only by careful planning. He denied being a painter of the unreal or abstract, as he explained: "For me, a form is never something abstract; it is always a sign of something. It is always a man, a bird, or something else. For me painting is never form for form's sake." Some people liken his art to that of Paul Klee. Compare for yourself.

Miró could master almost every medium. He worked with oil, gouache, and crayons on wood and canvas; he also applied bits of paper, cardboard, string, rope, metal, feathers, and plaster, to form exciting collages. He made pottery, sculpture, etchings, and woodcuts, designed costumes and scenery for the ballet, and illustrated books. He created large-scale murals in ceramic tile, such as his colorful *Walls of the Sun and the Moon* for the UNESCO Building in Paris, completed in 1959.

The Harlequin's Carnival. 1924–25. *In 1924, a movement called Surrealism was born, in which artists and writers sought to express thoughts of their subconscious mind through fantasy and dreams. And so they drew upon all the sources of their rich imaginations to create the symbols and forms to convey their strange messages. Miró, a leading Surrealist, here scattered ladders, eyes, ears, musical notes, and funny little creatures. With great skill he combined all the wiggling elements (which seem like magnified bacteria) into a carnival fantasy.*

Moore *Born 1898*

HENRY MOORE IS ONE of the leading sculptors of the twentieth century. "A sculptor," he once said, "is a person who is interested in the shape of . . . anything and everything . . . animals, people, pebbles. . . . All things . . . can help you to make sculpture."

His first ideas no doubt came from the wide fields and large, natural stone formations of his native Yorkshire, in England. His artistic talents showed by age twelve. He became a schoolteacher at eighteen, then served in World War I. After the war, he studied art on a soldier's grant, and at twenty-four won a sculpture scholarship in London. He haunted the British Museum, drawn there by the primitive Mexican sculptures and classical and medieval art. At twenty-seven he began to teach at the Royal College, and continued his work in sculpture and drawing.

Moore broke away from the art of his time in England to create exciting forms all his own. He took ideas from materials and their shapes, and made many small plaster models which he used for his large sculptures. He was always interested in themes of nature and life—mother and child, family groups, and the human figure in all types of poses. He explained: "I would like to think my sculpture has force, strength, life, vitality from *inside* it, so that you have a sense that the form is pressing from inside trying to burst . . . rather than having something which is just shaped from outside." He stresses the importance of bones pushing against the flesh from inside, at the skull, knee, shoulder—at all the vital points in his figures. He probes not so much for beauty as for the life force within the shape. This inner energy is the essence of Henry Moore's great sculpture.

Photograph of Henry Moore in his studio. Moore usually develops large works from small plaster models. He collects natural shapes—pieces of wood, bone, pebbles, shells—which form the basis for his ideas. As we see here, he prefers graceful, natural forms to sharp geometric shapes.

Family Group. 1945–49. *Moore sculpted many family groups showing the closeness of mother, father, and child as they face the world together. In creating this group, he made many drawings and models in different materials, both realistic and abstract in design. The three figures are formed like links in a chain, arms and legs interweaving in a firm unity.*

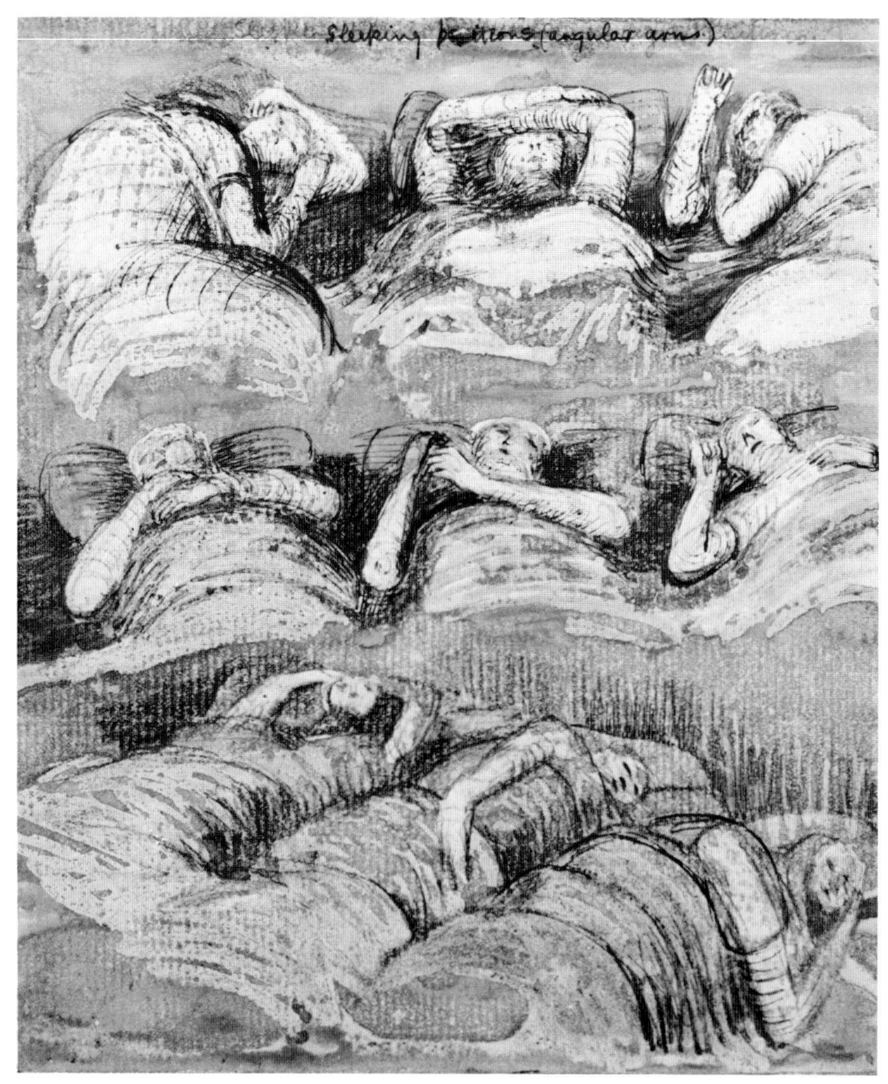

Sleeping Positions (*from* Shelter Sketchbook). 1941. *When London was bombed in World War II, thousands of people slept in underground railway stations. Moore drew them as they crowded in the dark caverns, showing harsh reality by dramatic groupings, accenting shapes and gestures as in his sculpture. These powerful drawings brought Moore his first real popularity.*

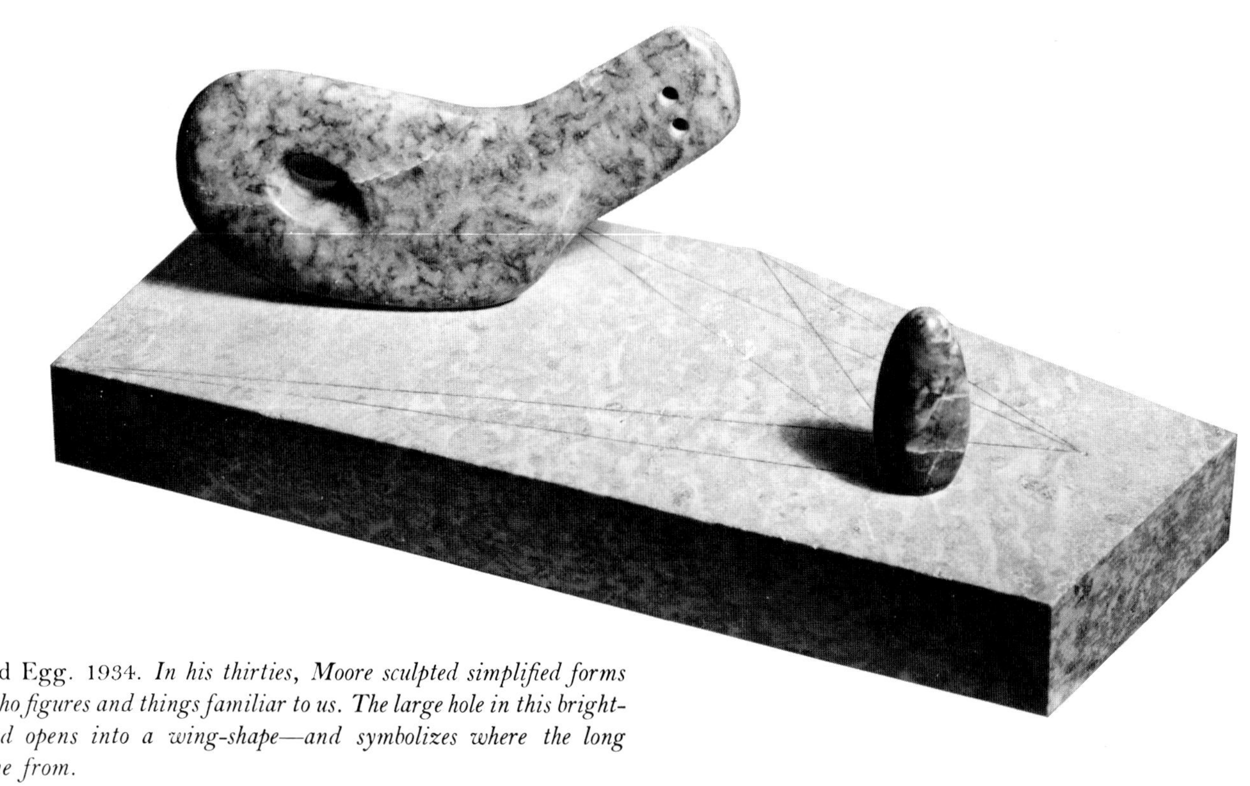

Bird and Egg. 1934. *In his thirties, Moore sculpted simplified forms which echo figures and things familiar to us. The large hole in this bright-eyed bird opens into a wing-shape—and symbolizes where the long egg came from.*

Moore CONTINUED

Reclining Figure. 1957–58. *For the new Paris headquarters of* UNESCO *(United Nations Educational, Scientific, and Cultural Organization), Moore did his largest work, sixteen and one-half feet long. To enrich the huge building with its walls of windows, he created a massive reclining figure, a favorite theme of which he made more than fifty variations. For this masterpiece, he first made a rough carving of the form right in the marble quarry near Rome. The marble was then moved to Paris, where Moore finished the work. Life seems to press strongly from within this mountainous form, and its force dominates the scene.*

De Kooning Born 1904

WILLEM DE KOONING WAS A LEADER of the New York School, which changed the direction of painting throughout the Western world in the 1950s. At the same time as Jackson Pollock, he helped to develop the movement called Abstract Expressionism, or Action Painting—the explosive, emotional rendering of the artist's personal world in abstract, random patterns and designs. About the exploding violence in his work, De Kooning said: "Art never seems to make me peaceful and pure. I do not think . . . of art, in general, as a situation of comfort."

A native of Rotterdam, Holland, De Kooning left school at twelve to work for commercial artists and decorators. At night, during the next eight years, the eager youngster studied anatomy, drawing, and color theory at an art academy. At twenty-two, De Kooning moved to New York. There he took a studio, and he enjoyed contact with other struggling young people in the arts. To earn a living, he did odd jobs for decorators and painted murals for restaurants. Finally, in 1936, employed by the Federal Arts Project, he was able to paint full time and so began to develop his personal expression and to help create a living American art.

He worked in two seemingly opposite directions: careful, realistic figure painting, and unrecognizable abstract forms. His art was applauded by other adventurous painters, but not by buyers. Still, his first one-man show in 1948 (which included exciting abstractions done in house paints, because he could not afford oils) aroused critical praise, and he soon became the successful leader of a new movement. He taught art at Black Mountain College and Yale University, and held major exhibitions in the 1950s and 1960s. He continued to break up and reassemble forms with a passion like that of Van Gogh.

De Kooning was seeking new ways to picture not what the eye sees but what the artist *feels*, and to express this

Easter Monday. 1956. *Working with the figure became "too terrible" for De Kooning, and in the late 1950s he entered a new abstract period. He continued to brush and spatter paint on the canvas, producing violent movement within a unified composition. Here he transferred newspaper images to the canvas, then painted over them in oil. Such abstract pictures emerged from long, hard work and intense inner struggle.*

◀ OPPOSITE PAGE

Woman I. 1950–52. *This painting is a landmark of art of the 1950s. De Kooning painted this canvas, then scraped it, made changes, and tossed it aside. Attacking it again, he cut parts out of some of his drawings, pasted them on the canvas, and painted over them. After two years' work, the result was a new, savage kind of representation—a nightmare vision, shocking even to the artist. He masterfully forced the violent elements of color, line, and form to work in tense unity, holding the explosive forms together and yet creating an unusual sensation of seeing more than one depth at the same time. About his famous series,* Women, *De Kooning said: "I always started out with the idea . . . of a beautiful woman. . . . I didn't mean to make them such monsters."*

through the patterns and forms created in the very *action* of painting. But expressing his feelings through painting was very difficult. Always dissatisfied, De Kooning would work over his canvases again and again, even destroying many works. He painted directly on canvas without sketches, letting each step guide him to the next. He returned to the human form for subject matter. He painted a series of *Women* in the early 1950s, returned to abstraction, then turned again to *Women* in the 1960s. Gradually his forms became simpler, his brush strokes larger, and his colors fresher. This constant change is the essence of his art.

Working Man. About 1938. *Other artists praised De Kooning's talent for fine drawing long before he gained fame. A simple directness and delicacy of line give this drawing an unusual sensitivity, and reveal the sad humble character of the worker, particularly in the large, dark eyes.*

Painting. 1948. *In his late thirties, De Kooning painted a group of black-and-white abstractions. He made black shapes like smooth, flat slabs of stone, separated by lively white lines. These challenging works were shown in his first one-man exhibition in New York, and marked him as an important artist and a leader in the growing movement of Abstract Expressionism.*

Reclining Figure in Marsh Landscape. 1967. *In the 1960s, the artist again returned to his series of* Women, *but without his earlier frantic struggle (as in* Woman I). *Many of these later paintings are very colorful and freely brushed. Here, although the figure is not at all detailed, we find a massive form stretched diagonally across the lively canvas.*

Excavation. 1950. *De Kooning said his first inspiration for this painting came from a movie about people working in rice fields. He sought to paint the* feeling *of digging and throwing up dirt. The restless shapes and brush strokes seem about to burst out of the sides of the picture, forming a dense, surging atmosphere in which one can hardly breathe.*

Blue Poles. 1953. *One of his last canvases, this may be Pollock's greatest work. Here he used oils, glittering silver aluminum paints, and synthetic plastic paints to create brilliant colors in violent movement within a harmonious unity—a complex living surface, a personal universe. The poles may have been inspired by his interest in Indian totem poles. Pollock said of his work: "On the floor I am more at ease. I feel nearer, more a part of the painting, since I can walk around it . . . and literally be in the painting. . . . When I am in my painting, I'm not aware of what I'm doing. . . . I have no fears about making changes, destroying the image, etc., because the painting has a life of its own. I try to let it come through. It is only when I lose contact with the painting that the result is a mess. Otherwise there is pure harmony, an easy give and take, and the painting comes out well."*

Summertime. 1948. *One of a series of long, narrow paintings, this joyous work is a tumbling parade of colorful forms, expressing the gaiety of a bright summer day. Pollock's paintings of this time he called "drip paintings"—see how beautifully the lines are "dripped" over the canvas to form a continual, swirling pattern without beginning or end.*

Pollock 1912–1956

FEW ARTISTS have aroused as much controversy in their lifetime as did Jackson Pollock. He tried to wipe away the limitations of contemporary American art.

Born in Cody, Wyoming, Pollock spent his childhood in the West. He studied art first in a Los Angeles high school, then, after moving to New York, at the Art Students League. This traditional art instruction, he later said, gave him something to react against. And his reaction was indeed great, resulting in the formation of the revolutionary style called Action Painting—because his method involved the rather violent *action* of dribbling, splashing, and flinging paint onto the canvas.

This method was a totally new way of applying paint to a surface, and it met with severe criticism (Pollock was jeeringly called "Jack the Dripper"). But Pollock was really continuing in the direction of Expressionism first explored by Kandinsky. Pollock wanted his art to have its own abstract forms and to express his powerful emotions, his explosive personality.

Instead of following the styles of others, he experimented by first laying out the canvas on the floor; then, while moving quickly around the canvas, he flung paint in seemingly random splashes and dribbles. The very act of painting was his way of expressing himself. He tried to let his movements be directed by the unconscious thoughts of his mind, to lose himself in the painting and be unaware of what he was doing. He said: "I don't work from drawings or color sketches. . . . I want to express my feelings rather than illustrate them."

Pollock's search for self-expression was often hindered by agony and self-doubt. He had to endure poverty and criticism, and was laughed at by the public. Finally, his life was cut short by a tragic automobile accident when he was only forty-four. His art may confuse you, but these pictures came from knowledge and control developed through nearly thirty years of study and hard work. Pollock's personal way of thinking, seeing, and painting expressed his own inner *truth*.

One (Number 31). 1950. *Pollock painted* One *without a brush—he used a stick to trickle, drip, and throw paint, to weave a complex web of colors. He said: "I continue to get further away from the usual painter's tool such as easel, palette, brushes, etc. I prefer sticks, trowels, knives and dripping fluid paint or a heavy impasto with sand, broken glass, and other foreign matter added."*

Photograph of Pollock at work. Here we see Pollock creating an Action Painting. His frantic movements—throwing, pouring, and dribbling paint—were as graceful as those of a dancer. He seemed to be trying to release forces within the paint itself, with himself as the source of energy.

Pollock CONTINUED

Masqued Image. 1938. *Pollock's early work, largely representational, was vigorous and adventurous. Forms are recognizable—how many masks can you find? The masks and totem pole forms reflect his admiration for Mexican and Indian art.*

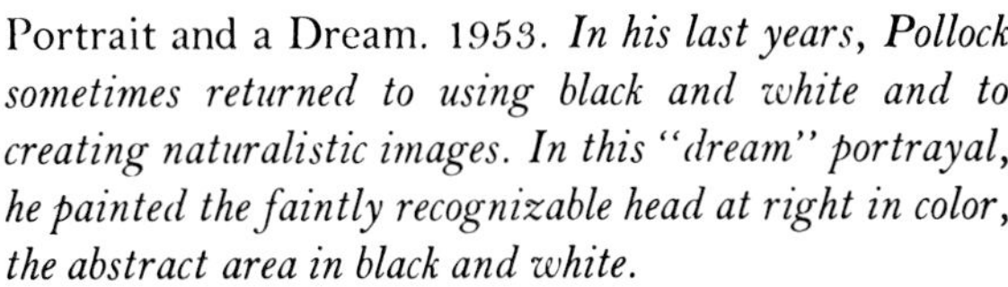

Portrait and a Dream. 1953. *In his last years, Pollock sometimes returned to using black and white and to creating naturalistic images. In this "dream" portrayal, he painted the faintly recognizable head at right in color, the abstract area in black and white.*

Glossary

ABSTRACT, ABSTRACTION. In art, the departure from natural appearances in order to create new arrangements of lines, colors, shapes, forms, and textures. Such arrangements are not very abstract when they strongly remind us of nature; but they may also be so abstract that there is no resemblance whatsoever. Geometrical abstract art reduces forms to solids such as cones, cylinders, cubes, and spheres; or to flat arrangements of lines, circles, and rectangles. Other forms of abstraction lead to irregular, freely invented shapes, colors, and movements, and their effect is more emotional.

ABSTRACT EXPRESSIONISM. See Action Painting.

ACADEMIC. Any style or movement following established rules of the leading art academies in particular periods.

ACTION PAINTING. A style of painting where paint is applied to the surface by splashing, dribbling, dripping, or by vigorous broad brush strokes and rapid lines placed more or less at random. The images resulting may then suggest further developments to the artist. But the final result is intended to be enjoyed for itself, since it does not represent anything. Like music, it may be quiet, boisterous, gay, somber, and so on, reflecting the artist's mood or feeling.

AFRICAN ART. African Negro art comes chiefly from the central part of Africa, extending from the west coast into the interior. Known to Europeans in the fifteenth century, African sculpture was brought to Europe in large quantities in the late nineteenth century and aroused great interest and attention. Ancestor and nature worship are important among the basic factors in shaping the styles of African art.

ANATOMY. The physical structure of a human, animal, or plant, or any of its parts.

ARCHITECTURE. The technique and art of building.

ART MOVEMENTS. Particular styles or tendencies that have been directed or formed through theories or shared methods of expression. Examples: Impressionism, Romanticism, Cubism.

ART PERIOD. An extensive span of time in which the art produced maintains characteristics that are recognizable as a unified style.

BAROQUE. The dominant style of art and architecture of the seventeenth and early eighteenth centuries in Europe. It is often characterized by dramatic subjects, rich ornamentation, and bold and twisting line movements with emphasis on strong action.

CANVAS. The surface on which an artist applies his paints, a heavy cloth made of linen or cotton. The word canvas is also used to refer to a finished picture on canvas cloth.

CARICATURE. A satire of a person, or a style, addiction, fad, and so on, visualized in painting, drawing, and sculpture through the exaggeration of defects or peculiarities of appearance or character.

CAST, CASTING. A sculptural process; a material such as liquid bronze is poured into a mold and allowed to harden.

CERAMICS. The art of making objects of clay and similar materials which are hardened by firing (a baking process).

CHIAROSCURO. The distribution of light and shade in a painting for dramatic effect (see Rembrandt).

CLASSIC, CLASSICAL. These terms usually refer to the style of Greek art during the fifth and fourth centuries B.C., which emphasized simplicity, harmony, proportion, discipline, and balance.

COLLAGE. A picture or design composed of a background on which are pasted materials such as colored papers, photographs, string, newspaper clippings, fabric, and so on. Sometimes the artist also paints or draws on the picture.

COMPOSITION. The arranging of the parts of a picture so as to create a satisfactory unity for the viewer.

CONTRAST. Strongly differing forms, lines, or

colors placed next to each other, such as black next to white.

Craftsman. A worker skilled in the use of tools and materials.

Cubism. An art movement of the early twentieth century in which the artist simplified the forms of the visual world into geometric shapes—cubes, cones, and rectangular planes. Whether the objects were near or distant they were handled in the same way, and each object was shown from more than one viewpoint (the front, side, and back views may appear at the same time).

Decoration. Ornamentation designed to beautify a surface.

Design. A controlled, rhythmic arrangement of lines, shapes, forms, textures, and colors.

Distortion. Usually an intentional change by the artist from the normal appearance, shape, or form of an object or image, such as twisting it or making it longer, serving to convey stronger feeling or improve the composition.

Draftsman. An artist skilled in the fundamentals of drawing.

Drawing. The process of representing what the artist sees, feels, or thinks about, on a two-dimensional surface, usually paper. Materials used include pencil, silverpoint on specially coated paper, pen and ink, brush and ink, charcoal, and various types of crayon, such as lithographic and conté crayon. Also, the finished product made by this process.

Engraving. A graphic art, involving the cutting of a drawing or design into a hard surface, such as a metal plate or block of wood. The design is then inked, the surface wiped clean, and the plate run through a press. The ink remaining in the cut areas imprints the drawing on paper. This process may be repeated many times to make any number of prints. Also, a print made by this process.

Etching. A graphic art, involving a slightly different process from engraving. Wax is spread over a metal plate; then a design or drawing is drawn into the surface with a special etching needle. The plate is dipped into acid which bites the design into the surface of the plate where it was etched, while the wax protects the rest. The wax is removed; the plate is then inked, wiped, and printed as described under Engraving. Also, a print made by this process.

Expressionism. A twentieth-century style, in which a painter stresses his inner personal feelings in his art. He often distorts or exaggerates forms derived from nature, and uses vivid colors for this purpose.

Fantasy. An image in the mind, as a daydream. A cleverly inventive thought or design.

Fauves. "Wild beasts," a name given in the early twentieth century to a group of French painters who used violent, vivid colors, bold brush strokes, and unconventional arrangements of forms, which did not necessarily describe realistically the subjects they painted.

Form. Refers to three-dimensional effects produced either by structural drawing or by surfaces that suggest depth and solidity. Descriptive terms are applied to form, such as basic, geometric, simplified, functional, expressive, complex, and free.

Fresco. Painting that involves the application of colors ground in water onto a wet plaster wall. The paint and the wall dry and harden together, forming a lasting surface.

Gouache. Pigment mixed with water, and thickened with gum arabic to make the color opaque (rather than transparent). Sometimes called tempera.

Graphic Arts. The arts of drawing and printmaking. Drawings may be in pencil, ink, or crayon, or other graphic media; prints are impressions made from specially prepared surfaces of wood, metal, or stone.

Harmony. A pleasing arrangement of the elements of a painting or sculpture.

Impressionism. A style of painting which began in France in the 1860s among artists who believed that light was the most important factor, and who tried to paint the qualities of light and atmosphere by placing next to each other short brush strokes of bright colors.

Landscape. A picture in which natural scenery is represented as the main theme, rather than simply as background.

Line. As used in drawing or painting, refers to the real or imaginary edges or outlines of objects, forms, or spaces. Qualities of line may be delicate or forceful, precise or vague, soft or hard, static or active, rhythmic or chaotic, flowing or jerky.

Lithography. A graphic art. First a drawing is made with a greasy crayon or ink on a specially prepared slab of limestone. The greasy areas are then fixed to stay on the stone, and it is washed with water. When the printing ink is rolled onto the stone, it remains only on the greasy areas, while the wet portions remain clean. Paper is then pressed on the stone, and picks up the ink from the greased pattern. For each color desired, a separate drawing is made on another stone. The colors are then printed one over the other.

Medium. The material, such as oil paint, watercolor, pastel, chalk, stone, clay, or wood, used by the artist to create his works of art. The plural is media or mediums.

Modeling. In sculpture, the shaping of forms. In drawing and painting, the creation of the illusion of solids on a flat surface.

Monumental. Massive or imposing, seemingly larger than life.

Mosaic. A technique in which small pieces of colored glass, stone, or other material are inlaid in an adhesive background material to form a pattern; also, a decoration made by this process.

Mural. A technique in which paint is applied directly onto a wall or, if on canvas, fastened to its surface by glue; also, a picture made by this process.

Neo-Impressionism. The theory and practice of painting with small dots or points of pure color, as devised by Georges Seurat.

Neo-Plasticism. A theory of utter simplicity in painting, devised by Piet Mondrian, who used the rectangle as the basic form, and limited his colors to black, white, red, yellow, and blue.

Old Master. An eminent artist of an earlier period, especially, in Europe, from the fifteenth through the eighteenth century.

Painting. The art of using a fluid medium for decoration of a flat surface, usually of canvas, wood, or plaster. Watercolor, oil, tempera, and synthetic paints are commonly used. Paintings may express depth, atmosphere, space, form, and movement through the use of color.

Pastels. Chalk-like sticks made from a dried paste ground with pigments and gum water, used to make drawings.

Pattern. Design created by a variety of dark and light values, through the interplay and contrast of colors.

Perspective. The technique of representing on a flat surface the position in space of objects as they appear to the eye. Linear perspective is based on the fact that receding parallel lines appear to meet at a single vanishing point. Atmospheric or aerial perspective suggests depth by diminishing the clarity and color of objects as they are increasingly distant from the eye.

Pigment. A colored substance (a mineral, stone, or chemical) in powdered form, which is mixed or ground with oil or water to make oil paints, watercolors, inks, crayons, and so on.

Polyptych. A work of art, such as an altarpiece, of two or more connected parts (see Triptych).

Portrait. A representation of a person, especially of a face.

Poster. A placard or bill intended for posting in a public place, as for advertising.

Post-Impressionism. A term used to describe the style of French painting following Impressionism. In contrast to Impressionism, it emphasized form, solidity, and structure, while still preserving the color qualities of Impressionism.

Primitive Art. Art produced in a society of an early stage of development; also, the work of an unschooled or naive artist (see Rousseau).

Realism. Representation of nature as it appears to the eye.

Relief. In sculpture, the result of carving, shaping, or stamping, so that the subject stands out from the flat surface which serves as its background.

Renaissance. The revival (literally, the "rebirth") of classical Greek and Roman culture, giving new direction to sculpture, painting, literature, architecture, and scholarship, beginning in Italy in the fourteenth century and continuing in Europe to the mid-sixteenth century.

REPRESENTATIONAL ART. Painting or sculpture which tries to reproduce the actual physical appearance of a subject.

ROMANTICISM. A representational style of art, begun in the early nineteenth century, which sought to appeal to human emotions through its depiction of unfamiliar or strange beauty in people, exotic lands, and in the drama of legends and historical themes.

SCULPTURE. The art of producing figures or objects in a sculptural medium. Also, the works made by this process. Sculpture may be carved in stone or wood, or modeled in clay or plaster. The latter kinds are made permanent by firing, or by casting in a metal, usually bronze. Relief sculpture remains attached to a surface.

SFUMATO. The practice (devised by Leonardo da Vinci) of blending and blurring light and dark tones to create a hazy or smoky effect.

SITTER. One who poses for a work of art, usually a portrait.

SKETCH. A rapid painting or drawing, usually without details, to be used as a draft for a finished painting or sculpture.

STILL LIFE. Subject matter that is inanimate, or "still," primarily fruit, flowers, bowls, bottles, statues, or small animals or fish, often arranged on a cloth or table.

STYLE. The characteristic manner in which an artist works, or a particular period in art.

SURREALISM. A style of twentieth-century painting considered "super-real" (going "beyond" Realism), portraying the personality of the artist and his unconscious thoughts, dreams, and fantasies (see Miró).

SYMBOLS. Shapes, forms, signs, images, or lines, used to represent abstract ideas.

TEMPERA. Pigment mixed with egg, sometimes the white, sometimes the yolk, to make an opaque medium. Also see Gouache.

TEXTURE. The suggestion by an artist of how a painted or sculpted material would feel if it were touched, such as rough, smooth, silky, soft, and so on.

THREE-DIMENSIONAL. Having, or seeming to have, in painting or sculpture, the dimension of depth as well as width and height.

TRADITION. Rules or methods of producing art that have been passed along from one generation to another. Some elements of tradition prove useful, workable, and valuable; unthinking use of tradition leads to convention and, at worst, mere imitation.

TRIPTYCH. A painting on a set of three panels or canvases, hinged together.

TWO-DIMENSIONAL. Having the dimensions of height and width only.

VARNISH. A preparation of dissolved resinous matter which, when applied to the surface of a painting, dries and leaves a hard, glossy, transparent coating.

WATERCOLOR. Pigment mixed with water; also, a painting made with watercolors.

WOODCUT. A graphic art process. Printing is made by using a wood block into which a design has been cut; the parts not to be printed are cut away, and the rest of the surface is inked and pressed on the paper. Also, a print made by this process.

List of Illustrations

50 3/8 × 42 1/8″. Stedelijk Museum, Amsterdam, The Netherlands

PAGES 96–99

HONORE DAUMIER

French, 1808–1879 (*dome*-YAY)

Circus Parade. About 1865. Pen and wash, 15 1/4 × 12 1/8″. Museum of Fine Arts, Budapest, Hungary

Don Quixote. About 1868. Oil on canvas, 18 1/8 × 12 5/8″. Neue Pinakothek, Munich, Germany

The Laundress. About 1860–62. Oil on wood, 19 1/4 × 13″. The Louvre, Paris, France

Self-Portrait. About 1853. Bronze, height 28 3/8″. Bibliothèque Nationale, Paris, France

Two Sculptors. About 1863–66. Oil on wood, 11 × 14″. The Phillips Collection, Washington, D.C.

PAGES 104–107

EDGAR DEGAS

French, 1834–1917 (*duh*-GAH)

Before the Performance. 1882–83. Oil on canvas, 19 1/4 × 25″. National Gallery of Scotland, Edinburgh, Scotland

The Dancing Class. 1880. Pastel on paper, 24 3/4 × 18 7/8″. Denver Art Museum, Denver, Colo.

Four Dancers and Scenery. About 1903. Pastel on paper, 33 × 28 3/4″. Private Collection.

Frieze of Dancers. About 1885–90. Oil on canvas, 27 3/4 × 79″. The Cleveland Museum of Art, Cleveland, Ohio. Gift of Hanna Fund, 1946

The Glass of Absinthe. 1876. Oil on canvas, 36 × 27″. The Louvre, Paris, France

The Little Fourteen-Year-Old Dancer. 1880. Wax, height 39 1/2″. Collection Mr. and Mrs. Paul Mellon, Washington, D.C.

Self-Portrait. 1855. Etching, 9 × 5 5/8″. The Art Institute of Chicago, Chicago, Ill. Fair Fund

Race Horses at Longchamp. About 1873–75. Oil on canvas, 12 × 15 3/4″. Museum of Fine Arts, Boston, Mass. S. A. Denio Collection

PAGES 200–203

WILLEM DE KOONING

Dutch, works in U.S.A., born 1904 (*duh*-KOON-*ing*)

Easter Monday. 1956. Oil and newspaper transfer on canvas, 96 × 74″. The Metropolitan Museum of Art, New York, N.Y. Rogers Fund, 1956

Excavation. 1950. Oil on canvas, 6′ 8 1/8″ × 8′ 4 1/8″. The Art Institute of Chicago, Chicago, Ill. Gift of Edgar Kaufmann and Mr. and Mrs. N. Goldowsky

Painting. 1948. Ripolin enamel and oil on canvas, 42 5/8 × 56 1/8″. The Museum of Modern Art, New York, N.Y.

Reclining Figure in Marsh Landscape. 1967. Oil on paper, 23 × 18 1/4″. Collection Mr. and Mrs. Jay Braus, New York, N.Y.

Woman I. 1950–52. Oil on canvas, 75 7/8 × 58″. The Museum of Modern Art, New York, N.Y.

Working Man. About 1938. Pencil drawing, 11 × 9″. Collection Max Margulis, New York, N.Y.

PAGES 92–95

EUGENE DELACROIX

French, 1798–1863 (*duh-la*-KRWAH)

Arab on Horseback Attacked by a Lion. 1849. Oil on canvas, 18 × 14 3/4″. The Art Institute of Chicago, Chicago, Ill. Potter Palmer Collection

Dante and Vergil in Hell (detail). 1822. Oil on canvas, 74 × 97″. The Louvre, Paris, France

Head of a Roaring Lion. About 1843. Watercolor, 7 × 7 5/8″. Cabinet des Dessins, The Louvre, Paris, France

Horse Attacked by Panther. About 1825. Watercolor, 7 × 10″. Cabinet des Dessins, The Louvre, Paris, France

Massacre of Chios. 1824. Oil on canvas, 13′ 8″ × 11′ 7″. The Louvre, Paris, France

Self-Portrait. 1837. Oil on canvas, 26 × 21″. The Louvre, Paris, France

Women of Algiers. 1834. Oil on canvas, 71 × 90″. The Louvre, Paris, France

PAGES 32–35

ALBRECHT DURER

German, 1471–1528 (DYU-*rer*)

The Four Apostles. 1526. Oil on wood, two panels, each 85 × 30″. Alte Pinakothek, Munich, Germany

The Four Horsemen of the Apocalypse. About 1497–98. Woodcut, 15 1/2 × 11 1/8″. The British Museum, London, England

The Great Clump of Turf. 1503. Watercolor and gouache, 16 1/8 × 12 1/2″. The Albertina, Vienna, Austria

Hare. 1502. Watercolor and gouache, 9 7/8 × 8 7/8″. The Albertina, Vienna, Austria

Head of a Roebuck. About 1503. Watercolor. Musée Bonnat, Bayonne, France

Self-Portrait. 1484. Silverpoint, 10 3/4 × 7 5/8″. The Albertina, Vienna, Austria

Self-Portrait. 1498. Oil on wood, 20 1/2 × 16 1/8″. The Prado, Madrid, Spain

Walrus. 1521. Drawing, 7 7/8 × 12 1/2″. The British Museum, London, England

PAGES 128–131

THOMAS EAKINS

American, 1844–1916 (AY-*kins*)

The Concert Singer (sketch). About 1892. Canvas mounted on wood, 14 3/8 × 10 3/8″. The Philadelphia Museum of Art, Philadelphia, Pa.

The Concert Singer—Portrait of Weda Cook (Mrs. Stanley Addicks). 1892. Oil on canvas, 75 × 54″. The Philadelphia Museum of Art, Philadelphia, Pa.

The Gross Clinic. 1875. Oil on canvas, 96×78″. Collection The Jefferson Medical College, Philadelphia, Pa. Courtesy of The Philadelphia Museum of Art.

Self-Portrait. 1902. Oil on canvas, 30×25″. Permanent Collection, National Academy of Design, New York, N.Y.

Walt Whitman. 1887. Oil on canvas, 30×24″. Pennsylvania Academy of the Fine Arts, Philadelphia, Pa.

PAGES 80–83

THOMAS GAINSBOROUGH

English, 1727–1788 (GAINS-*burr-oh*)

Blue Boy (Jonathan Buttall). About 1770. Oil on canvas, 70×48″. Henry E. Huntington Library and Art Gallery, San Marino, Calif.

The Honorable Mrs. Graham. 1775–76. Oil on canvas, 92 1/4×59 1/2″. National Gallery of Scotland, Edinburgh, Scotland

Robert Andrews and His Wife. About 1750. Oil on canvas, 27×47″. The National Gallery, London, England

Self-Portrait. About 1758–59. Oil on canvas, 30×25″. National Portrait Gallery, London, England

The Watering Place. About 1777. Oil on canvas, 58×71″. The National Gallery, London, England

PAGES 136–139

PAUL GAUGUIN

French, 1848–1903 (*go*-GAN)

Noa-Noa. 1895–1900. Watercolor. Cabinet des Dessins, The Louvre, Paris, France

Self-Portrait Dedicated to Vincent van Gogh (detail). 1888. Oil on canvas. Stedelijk Museum, Amsterdam, The Netherlands

The Spirit of the Dead Watches. 1892. Oil on canvas, 28 3/4×36 1/4″. Albright-Knox Art Gallery, Buffalo, N.Y. A. Conger Goodyear Collection

Still Life with Head-Shaped Vase and Japanese Woodcut. 1889. Oil on canvas, 28 1/2×36 1/2″. Collection Henry Ittleson, Jr., New York, N.Y.

Tahitian Landscape. 1891. Oil on canvas, 26 3/4×36 3/8″. The Minneapolis Institute of Arts, Minneapolis, Minn.

The Vision after the Sermon (Jacob Wrestling with the Angel). 1888. Oil on canvas, 28 3/4×36 1/4″. National Gallery of Scotland, Edinburgh, Scotland

PAGES 8–11

GIOTTO

Italian, about 1266–1337 (JAWT-*toh*)

Flight into Egypt. 1305–6. Fresco. Arena Chapel, Padua, Italy

The Lamentation over Christ (and detail). About 1305–6. Fresco. Arena Chapel, Padua, Italy

Saint Francis Gives His Cloak to a Poor Knight. About 1296–1300. Fresco. Church of San Francesco, Assisi, Italy

Supposed Self-Portrait (detail from *Last Judgment*). 1305–6. Fresco. Arena Chapel, Padua, Italy

PAGES 84–87

FRANCISCO GOYA

Spanish, 1746–1828 (GAW-*yah*)

And There Is No Remedy (from *The Disasters of War*). Begun 1808. Etching, 5 1/8×6 1/8″. The Metropolitan Museum of Art, New York, N.Y.

Don Manuel Osorio de Zuñiga. 1784. Oil on canvas, 50×40″. The Metropolitan Museum of Art, New York, N.Y. The Jules S. Bache Collection, 1949

The Executions of May 3, 1808, in Madrid. 1814–15. Oil on canvas, 8′ 9″×13′ 4″. The Prado, Madrid, Spain

Self-Portrait in a Tall Hat. About 1826. Oil on canvas, 23 3/4×18″. Kunsthistorisches Museum, Vienna, Austria

Two Old People Eating Soup. 1820–22. Oil on wood transferred to canvas, 20 7/8×33 1/2″. The Prado, Madrid, Spain

PAGES 56–59

EL GRECO

Born in Crete, worked in Spain, 1541–1614 (GRECK-*oh*)

Portrait of Don Fernando Niño de Guevara. About 1600. Oil on canvas, 67 1/4×42 1/2″. The Metropolitan Museum of Art, New York, N.Y. Bequest of Mrs. H. O. Havemeyer, 1929. The H. O. Havemeyer Collection

Saint John the Evangelist. About 1604. Oil on canvas, 35 1/4×30 3/8″. The Prado, Madrid, Spain

Saint Luke. About 1604. Oil on canvas, 38 5/8×30 3/4″. Cathedral, Toledo, Spain

The Saviour. About 1604. Oil on canvas, 39×31″. Cathedral, Toledo, Spain

Supposed Self-Portrait. About 1600–10. Oil on canvas, 23 1/4×18 1/4″. The Metropolitan Museum of Art, New York, N.Y. Joseph Pulitzer Bequest Fund, 1924

View of Toledo. About 1604–10. Oil on canvas, 47 3/4×42 3/4″. The Metropolitan Museum of Art, New York, N.Y. Bequest of Mrs. H. O. Havemeyer, 1929. The H. O. Havemeyer Collection

The Virgin with Saint Ines and Saint Tecla. About 1597–99. Oil on canvas, 76 1/8×40 1/2″. National Gallery of Art, Washington, D.C. Widener Collection

PAGES 64–67

FRANS HALS

Dutch, about 1580–1666 (HAHLS)

Boy with a Skull (sometimes called *Hamlet*). About 1625–28. Oil on canvas. Collection Sir Richard Proby, Peterborough, England

Portrait of a Man and His Wife. 1621. Oil on canvas, 57 1/8×66 1/2″. Rijksmuseum, Amsterdam, The Netherlands

Self-Portrait. About 1650. Oil on wood, 12 7/8×11″. The Metropolitan Museum of Art, New York, N.Y. Michael Friedsam Collection, 1931

The Women Regents of the Old Men's Home in Haarlem. 1664. Oil on canvas, 67×98″. Frans Hals Museum, Haarlem, The Netherlands

Yonker Ramp and His Sweetheart. 1623. Oil on canvas, 41 1/2 × 31 1/4". The Metropolitan Museum of Art, New York, N.Y. Bequest of Benjamin Altman, 1913

PAGES 48–51
HANS HOLBEIN THE YOUNGER
German, 1497–1543 (HOLE-*bine*)

Edward VI as Prince of Wales. 1538. Oil and tempera on wood, 22 1/8 × 17 3/8". National Gallery of Art, Washington, D.C. Mellon Collection

Erasmus of Rotterdam. 1523. Oil on wood, 16 1/2 × 12 1/2". The Louvre, Paris, France

Family of the Artist. 1528–29. Oil and tempera on paper mounted on wood, 30 1/4 × 25 1/4". Offentliche Kunstsammlung, Basel, Switzerland

The Hands of Erasmus. About 1523. Silverpoint drawing. Cabinet des Dessins, The Louvre, Paris, France

Henry VIII. 1540. Oil on wood, 32 1/2 × 29". National Gallery, Rome, Italy

The Peddler (from *The Dance of Death*). 1523–26. Woodcut, 2 5/8 × 2". The British Museum, London, England

Study for a Self-Portrait. 1542–43. Chalk drawing on paper, 9 × 7 1/8". Uffizi Gallery, Florence, Italy

PAGES 152–155
WASSILY KANDINSKY
Russian, worked in Germany and France, 1866–1944 (*kan*-DINN-*skee*)

Bavarian Mountains with Village. 1909. Oil on canvas, 26 3/4 × 36 5/8". Collection Richard S. Zeisler, New York, N.Y.

Black Lines, No. 189. 1913. Oil on canvas, 51 1/4 × 51 3/8". The Solomon R. Guggenheim Museum, New York, N.Y.

Composition VIII. 1923. Oil on canvas, 55 1/8 × 78 3/4". The Solomon R. Guggenheim Museum, New York, N.Y.

First Abstract Watercolor (Untitled). 1910. Watercolor and ink, 19 1/4 × 25". Collection Madame Nina Kandinsky, Neuilly-sur-Seine, France

No. 683. 1941. Oil and lacquer on canvas, 35 × 45 5/8". The Solomon R. Guggenheim Museum, New York, N.Y.

Small Pleasures. 1913. Oil on canvas, 43 1/4 × 47 1/4". The Solomon R. Guggenheim Museum, New York, N.Y.

Photograph of Kandinsky, Paris, 1935 (Photo by Hannes Beckmann, New York)

PAGES 168–171
PAUL KLEE
Swiss-German, 1879–1940 (KLAY)

Around the Fish. 1926. Oil on canvas, 18 3/8 × 25 1/8". The Museum of Modern Art, New York, N.Y. Abby Aldrich Rockefeller Fund

Burden. 1939. Pencil drawing, 11 1/2 × 8 1/4". Collection Felix Klee, Bern, Switzerland

Drawing for Plants, Soil, and Air. 1920. Pen and ink, 8 5/8 × 7 1/8". Paul Klee Foundation, Institute of Fine Arts, Bern, Switzerland

Elfenau, after Nature. 1898. Drawing, 3 3/8 × 4 3/4". Collection Felix Klee, Bern, Switzerland

Landscape with Yellow Birds. 1923. Watercolor on blackened ground, 14 × 17 3/8". Private collection, Switzerland

Lost in Thought (Self-Portrait). 1919. Pencil, paper, and board, 7 3/4 × 10 3/4". The Pasadena Art Museum, Pasadena, Calif. Bequest of the Galka E. Scheyer Estate

Still-Life. 1940. Oil on wood, 39 5/8 × 31 1/2". Collection Felix Klee, Bern, Switzerland

PAGES 172–175
FERNAND LEGER
French, 1881–1955 (*lay*-ZHAY)

The Card Players. 1917. Oil on canvas, 50 7/8 × 76". Kröller-Müller Museum, Otterlo, The Netherlands

The Great Parade. 1954. Oil on canvas, 9' 10" × 13' 1". The Solomon R. Guggenheim Museum, New York, N.Y.

The Staircase. 1913. Oil on canvas, 56 3/4 × 46 1/2". Kunsthaus, Zurich, Switzerland

Three Women (Le Grand Déjeuner). 1921. Oil on canvas, 72 1/4 × 99". The Museum of Modern Art, New York, N.Y. Mrs. Simon of the Guggenheim Fund

Photograph of Léger, about 1950 (Photo Galerie Louise Leiris, Paris)

PAGES 28–31
LEONARDO DA VINCI
Italian, 1452–1519 (*lay-oh*-NAR-*doh-dah*-VEEN-*chee*)

Baptism of Christ (detail). About 1470–72. Uffizi Gallery, Florence, Italy

Flying Machine. About 1495. Drawing. Institut de France, Paris, France

Mona Lisa. About 1503. Oil on wood, 30 1/4 × 21". The Louvre, Paris, France

Self-Portrait. About 1512. Red chalk, 13 × 8 1/4". Royal Library, Turin, Italy

Virgin of the Rocks. Unfinished, begun about 1483. Oil on wood, 74 5/8 × 47 1/4". The National Gallery, London, England

PAGES 100–103
EDOUARD MANET
French, 1832–1883 (*ma*-NAY)

A Bar at the Folies Bergère. 1881–82. Oil on canvas, 37 1/2 × 51". Courtauld Institute of Art, London, England

Boy with a Fife. 1866. Oil on canvas, 63 × 38". The Louvre, Paris, France

Don Mariano Camprubi. 1862. Oil on canvas. Collection Mr. and Mrs. Donald S. Stralem, New York, N.Y.

Portrait of Emile Zola. 1868. Oil on canvas, 57 1/8 × 44 7/8". The Louvre, Paris, France

Race Course at Longchamp, Paris. 1864. Oil on canvas,

17 1/4×33 1/4″. The Art Institute of Chicago, Chicago, Ill. Potter Palmer Collection

Self-Portrait with Palette. 1879. Oil on canvas, 32 5/8× 26 3/8″. Collection Mr. and Mrs. John L. Loeb, New York, N.Y.

PAGES 156–159

HENRI MATISSE

French, 1869–1954 (*ma*-TEECE)

Green Stripe (Portrait of Madame Matisse). 1905. Oil and tempera, 15 7/8×12 7/8″. Royal Museum of Fine Arts, Copenhagen, Denmark.

Decorative Figure on Ornamental Background. 1927. Oil on canvas, 51 1/2×38 3/8″. Musée National d'Art Moderne, Paris, France.

Lady in Blue. Early state, February 1937. Finished state, April 1937. Oil on canvas, 36 1/2×29″. Collection Mrs. John Wintersteen, Philadelphia, Pa.

Pineapple and Anemones. 1940. Oil on canvas, 28 1/2× 35 1/2″. Collection Mrs. Albert D. Lasker, New York, N.Y.

The Red Studio. 1911. Oil on canvas, 71 1/4×86 1/4″. The Museum of Modern Art, New York, N.Y. Mrs. Simon Guggenheim Fund

Self-Portrait. 1906. Oil on canvas, 55×46″. Royal Museum of Fine Arts, Copenhagen, Denmark

Tahitian Landscape. About 1935. Ink drawing. Whereabouts unknown

PAGES 36–39

MICHELANGELO BUONARROTI

Italian, 1475–1564 (*mickel*-AHN-*jel-oh*)

Anatomy Sketches: Studies for the Libyan Sibyl. About 1510. Red chalk drawing, 11 3/8×8 1/2″. The Metropolitan Museum of Art, New York, N.Y. Purchase, 1924, Joseph Pulitzer Bequest

The Creation of Man (portion, from *The Sistine Chapel Ceiling*). 1511. Fresco. The Sistine Chapel, The Vatican, Rome, Italy

David. 1501–4. Marble, height 14′ 3″. Academy, Florence, Italy

Florentine Pietà. About 1548–56. Marble, height 92″. Cathedral, Florence, Italy

Pietà. 1498–99. Marble, height 69″. St. Peter's, The Vatican, Rome, Italy

The Sistine Chapel Ceiling (portion). About 1511–12. Fresco. The Sistine Chapel, The Vatican, Rome, Italy

PAGES 192–195

JOAN MIRO

Spanish, works in France, born 1893 (*mee*-ROH)

The Harlequin's Carnival. 1924–25. Oil on canvas, 25 1/4× 35 7/8″. Albright-Knox Art Gallery, Buffalo, N.Y.

L'Hirondelle d'Amour. 1934. Oil on canvas, 78 1/2× 97 1/2″. The Museum of Modern Art, New York, Gift of Nelson A. Rockefeller

Self-Portrait. 1937–38. Pencil, crayon, and oil on canvas, 57 1/2×38 1/4″. Collection James Thrall Soby, New Canaan, Conn.

Vegetable Garden with Donkey. 1918. Oil on canvas, 25 1/4×27 3/4″. Collection Mr. and Mrs. Irwin Shapiro, New York, N.Y.

Women and Birds in Front of the Sun. 1942. Gouache and pastel, 42 3/4×30 3/4″. The Art Institute of Chicago, Chicago, Ill. Wirt D. Walker Fund

PAGES 184–187

AMEDEO MODIGLIANI

Italian, worked in France, 1884–1920

(*mo-dee-lee*-AH-*nee*)

Bride and Groom. 1915–16. Oil on canvas, 21 3/4×18 1/4″. The Museum of Modern Art, New York, N.Y. Gift of Frederic Clay Bartlett

Head of a Woman. About 1910. Limestone, height 25 1/2″. National Gallery of Art, Washington, D.C. Chester Dale Collection

Little Girl in Blue. 1918. Oil on canvas, 46 1/8×28 1/2″. Private collection, Paris, France

The Little Peasant. 1918. Oil on canvas, 39 3/8×25 3/8″. The Tate Gallery, London, England

Lola de Valence. 1916. Oil on canvas, 20×13″. The Metropolitan Museum of Art, New York, N.Y. Bequest of Miss Adelaide Milton de Groot, 1967

Portrait of Jeanne Hébuterne. 1919. Oil on canvas, 51 1/4× 32″. Collection Mr. and Mrs. Sidney F. Brody, Los Angeles, Calif.

Self-Portrait. 1919. Oil on canvas, 33 1/2×23 1/2″. Museu de Arte Contemporânea da Universidade de São Paolo, Brazil

PAGES 164–167

PIET MONDRIAN

Dutch, worked in France and U.S.A., 1872–1944

(MOHN-*dree-ahn*)

Broadway Boogie-Woogie. 1942–43. Oil on canvas, 50× 50″. The Museum of Modern Art, New York, N.Y.

Composition with Red, Blue, and Yellow. 1930. Oil on canvas, 20×20″. Collection Mr. and Mrs. Armand P. Bartos, New York, N.Y.

Chrysanthemums. About 1908–10. Oil on canvas, 17 3/4× 12 5/8″. Gemeentemuseum, The Hague, The Netherlands. On loan from S. B. Slijper

Flowering Appletree. 1912. Oil on canvas, 30 3/4×41 3/4″. Gemeentemuseum, The Hague, The Netherlands

The Gray Tree. 1911. Oil on canvas, 31×42 3/8″. Gemeentemuseum, The Hague, The Netherlands

The Red Tree. 1909–10. Oil on canvas, 27 1/2×39″. Gemeentemuseum, The Hague, The Netherlands

Self-Portrait. 1918. Oil on canvas, 34 3/4×28 3/4″. Gemeentemuseum, The Hague, The Netherlands. On loan from S.B. Slijper

Victory Boogie-Woogie (sketch). About 1943. Pencil drawing, 19 1/4″ on the diagonal. Collection Harry Holtzman, Lime, Conn.

Victory Boogie-Woogie. 1943–44. Oil on canvas, 49 5/8 × 49 5/8″ on the diagonal. Collection Mr. and Mrs. Burton Tremaine, Meriden, Conn.

PAGES 112–115

CLAUDE MONET

French, 1840–1926 (*moh*-NAY)

Gare Saint-Lazare. 1877. Oil on canvas, 32 1/2 × 39 3/4″. Fogg Art Museum, Harvard University, Cambridge, Mass. Maurice Wertheim Collection

Impression: Sunrise. 1872. Oil on canvas, 19 5/8 × 25 1/2″. Musée Marmottan, Paris, France

Rouen Cathedral, Early Morning. 1892. Oil on canvas, 42 × 29″. Museum of Fine Arts, Boston, Mass. Tompkins Collection

Rouen Cathedral, Midday. 1894. Oil on canvas, 42 × 28 3/4″. The Louvre, Paris, France

Rouen Cathedral, Sunset. 1894. Oil on canvas, 39 1/2 × 25 3/4″. Museum of Fine Arts, Boston, Mass. Juliana Cheney Edwards Collection

Water Lilies. About 1918. Oil on canvas, 59 1/4 × 79″. Private Collection.

Women in the Garden. 1866–67. Oil on canvas, 8′ 4 1/2″ × 6′ 8 3/4″. The Louvre, Paris, France

Portrait of Monet by Manet. 1880. Pen and ink, 5 1/2 × 4 3/4″. Collection Mr. Robert von Hirsch, Basel, Switzerland

PAGES 196–199

HENRY MOORE

English, born 1898 (MOOR)

Bird and Egg. 1934. Marble. Collection Mr. and Mrs. Paul Mellon, Washington, D.C.

Family Group. 1945–49. Bronze, height 59 1/4″. The Museum of Modern Art, New York, N.Y. A. Conger Goodyear Fund

Reclining Figure. 1957–58. Marble, length 16′ 8″. UNESCO, Paris, France

Sleeping Positions (from *Shelter Sketchbook*). 1941. Pen, chalk, and wash, 8 × 6 1/2″. Collection Mrs. Irina Moore, Much Hadham, England

Photograph of Moore in his studio (Photo Mrs. Irina Moore, England)

PAGES 176–179

PABLO PICASSO

Spanish, works in France, born in 1881 (*pi*-KAH-*so*)

Baboon and Young. 1951. Bronze, height 21″. The Museum of Modern Art, New York, N.Y. Mrs. Simon Guggenheim Fund

Bullfight. 1957. Ink on paper, 19 3/4 × 25 3/4″. Galerie Louise Leiris, Paris, France

The Dream. 1932. Oil on canvas, 51 × 38 1/2″. Collection Mr. and Mrs. Victor W. Ganz, New York, N.Y.

Guernica. 1937. Oil on canvas, 11′ 6″ × 25′ 8″. On extended loan to the Museum of Modern Art, New York, N.Y., from the Artist

Les Demoiselles d'Avignon. 1906–7. Oil on canvas, 96 × 92″. The Museum of Modern Art, New York, N.Y. Acquired through the Lillie P. Bliss Bequest

Portrait of Daniel-Henry Kahnweiler. 1910. Oil on canvas, 39 5/8 × 28 5/8″. The Art Institute of Chicago, Chicago, Ill. Gift of Mrs. Gilbert W. Chapman

Self-Portrait. 1906. Oil on canvas, 36 1/2 × 28 3/4″. The Philadelphia Museum of Art, Philadelphia, Pa. A. E. Gallatin Collection

The Three Musicians. 1921. Oil on canvas, 6′ 7″ × 7′ 3 3/4″. The Museum of Modern Art, New York, N.Y. Mrs. Simon Guggenheim Fund

Woman with a Fan. 1905. Oil on canvas, 39 3/4 × 32 1/4″. National Gallery of Art, Washington, D. C., Gift of the W. Averell Harriman Foundation in memory of Marie N. Harriman

PAGES 16–19

PIERO DELLA FRANCESCA..

Italian, about 1415–1492

(*pee*-AIR-*oh-del-luh-fran*-CHESS-*kuh*)

The Duke and Duchess of Urbino. 1465. Oil on wood, two panels, each 18 1/2 × 13″. Uffizi Gallery, Florence, Italy

Geometric Head Designs—Front and Profile (from *De Prospectiva Pingendi*). About 1480. Biblioteca Palatina, Parma, Italy

King Solomon Receiving the Queen of Sheba. 1452–59. Fresco. Church of San Francesco, Arezzo, Italy

The Queen of Sheba. 1452–59. Fresco. Church of San Francesco, Arezzo, Italy

The Resurrection. About 1463. Fresco. Picture Gallery, Borgo San Sepolcro, Italy

The Victory of Heraclius over Chosroes. 1452–59. Fresco. Church of San Francesco, Arezzo, Italy

PAGES 204–207

JACKSON POLLOCK

American, 1912–1956 (PAHL-*uk*)

Blue Poles. 1953. Oil on canvas, 6′ 11″ × 16′. Australian National Gallery, Canberra

Masqued Image. 1938. Oil on canvas, 40 × 24″. Collection Lee Krasner Pollock. Courtesy of Marlborough-Gerson Gallery, New York

One (Number 31). 1950. Oil and enamel on canvas, 8′ 10″ × 17′ 5″. The Museum of Modern Art, New York, N.Y. Gift of Sidney Janis

Portrait and a Dream. 1953. Enamel on canvas, 4′ 10 1/4″ × 11′ 2 1/2″. Dallas Museum of Fine Arts, Dallas, Tex. Gift of Mr. and Mrs. Algur H. Meadows and the Meadows Foundation, Inc.

Summertime. 1948. Oil on canvas, 2′ 9 1/4″ × 18′3″. Collection Lee Krasner Pollock. Courtesy of Marlborough-Gerson Gallery, New York

Photograph of Pollock in his studio in East Hampton, Long Island (Photo by Hans Namuth, New York)

PAGES 40–43

RAPHAEL

Italian, 1483–1520 (RAFF-*e-ul*)

The Casa Tempi Madonna. 1505–6. Oil on wood, 29 1/2 × 20 1/8″. Alte Pinakothek, Munich, Germany

Saint George Slaying the Dragon. About 1512. Oil on wood, 12 1/4 × 10 5/8″. The Louvre, Paris, France

The School of Athens (and detail of Plato and Aristotle). 1511. Fresco. Stanza della Segnatura, Vatican Palace, Rome, Italy

Self-Portrait. About 1506. Oil on panel, 17 3/4 × 13″. Uffizi Gallery, Florence, Italy

PAGES 72–75

REMBRANDT VAN RIJN

Dutch, 1606–1669 (REM-*brant*)

A Cottage among Trees. About 1648. Pen and bister, 6 3/4 × 10 7/8″. The Metropolitan Museum of Art, New York, N.Y. Bequest of Mrs. H. O. Havemeyer, 1929. The H. O. Havemeyer Collection

Jacob Blessing the Sons of Joseph. 1656. Oil on canvas, 68 1/2 × 83 1/2″. Gemäldegalerie, Kassel, Germany

The Polish Rider. About 1655. Oil on canvas, 46 × 53 1/8″. Copyright The Frick Collection, New York, N.Y.

Self-Portrait. 1629. Oil on wood, 35 × 29″. Isabella Stewart Gardner Museum, Boston, Mass.

Self-Portrait. 1650. Oil on canvas, 36 1/4 × 29 3/4″. National Gallery of Art, Washington, D.C. Widener Collection

Self-Portrait. About 1656. Oil on wood, 20 × 16″. Kunsthistorisches Museum, Vienna, Austria

Self-Portrait. 1659. Oil on canvas, 33 1/4 × 26″. National Gallery of Art, Washington, D.C. Mellon Collection

Self-Portrait. 1660. Oil on canvas, 31 5/8 × 26 1/2″. The Metropolitan Museum of Art, New York, N.Y. Bequest of Benjamin Altman, 1913

Self-Portrait. 1663. Oil on canvas, 45 × 38″. The Iveagh Bequest, Kenwood, London, England

PAGES 120–123

PIERRE-AUGUSTE RENOIR

French, 1841–1919 (*renn*-WAHR)

Ballet Dancer. 1874. Oil on canvas, 56 1/8 × 37 1/8″. National Gallery of Art, Washington, D.C. Widener Collection

A Girl with a Watering Can. 1876. Oil on canvas, 39 1/2 × 28 3/4″. National Gallery of Art, Washington, D.C. Chester Dale Collection

Her First Evening Out. About 1880. Oil on canvas, 25 1/2 × 19 3/4″. The National Gallery, London, England

The Judgment of Paris. 1916. Bronze, 30 × 36 1/4″. Collection Dr. and Mrs. Harry Bakwin, New York, N.Y.

Madame Tilla Durieux. 1914. Oil on canvas, 36 1/2 × 29″. The Metropolitan Museum of Art, New York, N.Y. Bequest of Stephen C. Clark, 1960

Mademoiselle Romaine Lacaux. 1864. Oil on canvas, 32 × 25 1/2″. Cleveland Museum of Art, Cleveland, Ohio. Gift of Hanna Fund, 1942

Self-Portrait. 1910. Oil on canvas, 18 × 15″. Collection Durand-Ruel, Paris, France

Siesta. 1888. Drawing in sanguine, 12 × 9″. Cleveland Museum of Art, Cleveland, Ohio. John L. Severance Fund

Two Little Circus Girls. 1875–76. Oil on canvas, 51 1/2 × 38 1/2″. The Art Institute of Chicago, Chicago, Ill. Potter Palmer Collection

PAGES 116–119

AUGUSTE RODIN

French, 1840–1917 (*roh*-DAN)

The Burghers of Calais. 1884–86. Bronze, 82 5/8 × 94 1/2″. Rodin Museum, Paris, France

Cambodian Dancer. 1906. Wash drawing on paper, 16 7/8 × 11 3/8″. City Art Museum of St. Louis, Mo.

Monument to Balzac. 1893–98. Bronze, height 9′ 10″. Boulevard Raspail, Paris, France

Self-Portrait. 1859. Drawing. Musée du Petit Palais, Paris, France

Study Head for the Statue of Balzac. 1891–92. Bronze. Rodin Museum, Philadelphia, Pa. Courtesy of the Philadelphia Museum of Art

Study Head for the Statue of Balzac. About 1891–92. Terra cotta, height 9 1/2″. The Metropolitan Museum of Art, New York, N.Y. Rogers Fund, 1910

Study Head for the Statue of Balzac. About 1891–92. Plaster. Rodin Museum, Paris, France

The Thinker. 1880. Bronze, height 78 3/4″. The Metropolitan Museum of Art, New York, N.Y. Gift of Thomas F. Ryan, 1910

PAGES 160–163

GEORGES ROUAULT

French, 1871–1958 (*roo*-OH)

Joan of Arc. 1951. Oil on canvas, 11 3/4 × 9 1/2″. Private collection, Paris, France

The Old King. 1916–38. Oil on canvas, 30 1/4 × 21 1/4″. Museum of Art, Carnegie Institute, Pittsburgh, Pa.

The Poor Family (Exodus). About 1911. Oil on canvas, 25 3/4 × 19 3/4″. Musée de l'Annonciade, Saint-Tropez, France

Self-Portrait (Workman's Apprentice). 1925. Oil on canvas, 26 × 20 1/2″. Musée National d'Art Moderne, Paris, France

The Wounded Clown. 1932. Oil on canvas, 78 3/4 × 47 1/4". Private collection, Paris, France

PAGES 124–127
HENRI ROUSSEAU
French, 1844–1910 (*roo*-SO)

The Cart of Père Juniet. 1908. Oil on canvas, 38 1/4 × 50 3/4". The Louvre, Paris, France. Collection Jean Walter–Paul Guillaume

The Dream. 1910. Oil on canvas, 6' 8 1/2" × 9' 9 1/2". The Museum of Modern Art, New York, N.Y. Gift of Nelson A. Rockefeller

Lotus Flowers. 1910. Oil on canvas, 18 1/8 × 15". Collection Galerie Gattlen, Lausanne, Switzerland

Myself: Portrait-Landscape. 1890. Oil on canvas, 56 × 43". National Museum, Prague, Czechoslovakia

The Sleeping Gypsy. 1897. Oil on canvas, 51 × 79". The Museum of Modern Art, New York, N.Y. Gift of Mrs. Simon Guggenheim

PAGES 60–63
PETER PAUL RUBENS
Flemish, 1577–1640 (ROO-*bens*)

The Adoration of the Magi. 1624. Oil on wood, 14' 8" × 7' 8 1/2". Musée des Beaux-Arts, Antwerp, Belgium

The Artist's Sons, Albert and Nicholas. 1624–25. Oil on wood, 62 1/4 × 32 1/4". Liechtenstein Collection, Vaduz, Liechtenstein

Rubens and His First Wife. 1609–10. Oil on canvas, 69 1/2 × 53 1/2". Alte Pinakothek, Munich, Germany

Studies of Cattle. Drawing. Devonshire Collection, Chatsworth, England. Reproduced by permission of the Trustees of the Chatsworth Settlement

Wolf and Fox Hunt. About 1615. Oil on canvas, 8' × 12' 4 1/2". The Metropolitan Museum of Art, New York, N.Y. Kennedy Fund, 1910

PAGES 132–135
ALBERT PINKHAM RYDER
American, 1847–1917 (RYE-*der*)

Dead Bird. 1890–1900. Oil on wood, 4 1/4 × 9 7/8". The Phillips Collection, Washington, D.C.

The Forest of Arden. 1897. Oil on canvas, 19 × 15". The Metropolitan Museum of Art, New York, N.Y. Bequest of Stephen C. Clark, 1960

Moonlight Marine. 1870–90. Oil on wood, 11 3/8 × 12". The Metropolitan Museum of Art, New York, N.Y. Samuel D. Lee Fund, 1934

The Race Track. 1895–1910. Oil on canvas, 27 3/4 × 35 1/8". The Cleveland Museum of Art, Cleveland, Ohio. J. H. Wade Collection

Self-Portrait. About 1880. Oil on canvas, 6 × 4 1/2". Collection Mr. and Mrs. Lawrence Fleischmann, New York, N.Y.

PAGES 144–147
GEORGES SEURAT
French, 1859–1891 (*sir*-AH)

La Parade (Invitation to the Side Show). 1889. Oil on canvas, 39 1/2 × 59 1/2". The Metropolitan Museum of Art, New York, N.Y. Bequest of Stephen C. Clark, 1960

Port-en-Bessin, Entrance to the Harbor. 1888. Oil on canvas, 21 5/8 × 25 5/8". The Museum of Modern Art, New York, N.Y. Lillie P. Bliss Collection

The Steamboat. About 1886. Drawing, 9 3/8 × 12 1/8". Albright-Knox Art Gallery, Buffalo, N.Y. Gift of A. Conger Goodyear

Sunday Afternoon on the Island of La Grande Jatte (and detail). 1883–86. Oil on canvas, 6' 9" × 10' 6". The Art Institute of Chicago, Chicago, Ill. Helen Birch Bartlett Memorial Collection

Portrait of Seurat by Ernest Laurent. 1883. Drawing, 15 1/4 × 11 1/2". Musée National d'Art Moderne, Paris, France

PAGES 44–47
TITIAN
Italian, about 1490–1576 (TISH-*un*)

A Bacchanal (The People of Andros). About 1519. Oil on canvas, 66 7/8 × 76". The Prado, Madrid, Spain

The Entombment. 1559. Oil on canvas, 53 7/8 × 68 7/8". The Prado, Madrid, Spain

Portrait of Clarissa Strozzi. 1542. Oil on canvas, 45 1/4 × 38 5/8". Staatliche Museen, Berlin, Germany

Saint Sebastian. 1522. Oil on canvas, 66 7/8 × 25 5/8". Church of Saints Nazzaro and Celso, Brescia, Italy

Study for *Saint Sebastian.* 1520–22. Drawing, 6 1/2 × 5 1/4". Kupferstichkabinett, Staatliche Museen, Berlin, Germany

Study for *Saint Sebastian.* 1520–22. Drawing, 7 1/8 × 5". Städelsches Kunstinstitut, Frankfurt, Germany

Self-Portrait (section). About 1562. Oil on canvas. The Prado, Madrid, Spain

PAGES 148–151
HENRI DE TOULOUSE-LAUTREC
French, 1864–1901 (*too*-LOOZ-*low*-TREK)

At the Moulin Rouge. 1890. Oil on canvas, 45 × 59". Collection Henry P. McIlhenny, Philadelphia, Pa.

Divan Japonais. 1892. Lithograph, 31 7/8 × 24 5/8". The Museum of Modern Art, New York, N.Y.

In the Circus Fernando: The Ring Master. 1888. Oil on canvas, 39 1/2 × 63 1/2". The Art Institute of Chicago, Chicago, Ill. Joseph Winterbotham Collection

Monsieur Boileau in a Café. 1893. Gouache on cardboard, 31 1/2 × 25 5/8". The Cleveland Museum of Art, Cleveland, Ohio. Hinman B. Hurlbut Collection

Self-Portrait. Drawing. Whereabouts unknown

Photograph of Toulouse-Lautrec. About 1890. (Bibliothèque Nationale, Paris)

PAGES 88–91

JOSEPH MALLORD WILLIAM TURNER

English, 1775–1851 (TUR-*ner*)

Burning of the Houses of Parliament. 1835. Oil on canvas, 36 1/2 × 48 1/2″. The Cleveland Museum of Art, Cleveland, Ohio

San Giorgio from the Dogana, Venice: Sunrise. 1819. Watercolor, 8 3/4 × 12″. The British Museum, London, England

Self-Portrait. About 1798. Oil on canvas, 29 × 23″. The Tate Gallery, London, England

Snow Storm. 1842. Oil on canvas, 36 × 48″. The National Gallery, London, England

George IV at a Banquet in Edinburgh. 1822. Oil on wood, 26 1/4 × 35 1/2″. The Tate Gallery, London, England

PAGES 12–15

JAN VAN EYCK

Flemish, about 1390–1441 (*van*-IKE)

Giovanni Arnolfini and His Bride. 1434. Oil on wood, 33 × 22 1/2″. The National Gallery, London, England

Man in a Red Turban. 1433. Oil on wood, 10 1/4 × 7 1/2″. The National Gallery, London, England

Saint Barbara. 1437. Brush drawing, 12 3/4 × 7 1/4″. Musée des Beaux-Arts, Antwerp, Belgium

Virgin Mary and Crown (detail from the *Ghent Altarpiece*). About 1424–32. Oil on wood, 65 × 28″. St. Bavo, Ghent, Belgium

PAGES 140–143

VINCENT VAN GOGH

Dutch, worked in France, 1853–1890 (*van*-GO)

Crows over the Wheat Field. 1890. Oil on canvas, 19 7/8 × 39 1/2″. Stedelijk Museum, Amsterdam, The Netherlands

"La Mousmé." 1888. Oil on canvas, 28 7/8 × 23 3/4″. National Gallery of Art, Washington, D.C. Chester Dale Collection

Self-Portrait with Cut Ear. 1889. Oil on canvas, 20 1/2 × 18″. Collection Mr. and Mrs. Leigh B. Block, Chicago, Ill.

Starry Night. 1889. Pencil, 18 1/2 × 24 3/8″. Formerly Kunsthalle, Bremen, Germany (destroyed)

Sunflowers. 1888. Oil on canvas, 37 3/8 × 28 3/4″. The National Gallery, London, England

PAGES 68–71

DIEGO VELAZQUEZ

Spanish, 1599–1660 (*vuh*-LAHS-*kus*)

The Infanta Margarita. About 1653. Oil on canvas, 50 3/8 × 39 3/8″. Kunsthistorisches Museum, Vienna, Austria

The Infanta Margarita. About 1655. Oil on canvas, 27 1/2 × 23 1/4″. The Louvre, Paris, France

The Infanta Margarita. About 1656. Oil on canvas, 41 1/4 × 34 1/4″. Kunsthistorisches Museum, Vienna, Austria

King Philip IV at Fraga. 1644. Oil on canvas, 51 1/8 × 39 1/8″. Copyright The Frick Collection, New York

The Maids of Honor (Las Meninas). 1656. Oil on canvas, 10′ 5″ × 9′. The Prado, Madrid, Spain

Prince Balthasar Carlos on Horseback. About 1634. Oil on canvas, 82 1/4 × 68 1/8″. The Prado, Madrid, Spain

Prince Balthasar Carlos. About 1640–42. Oil on canvas, 50 3/8 × 39″. Kunsthistorisches Museum, Vienna, Austria

Prince Felipe Prosper. 1659. Oil on canvas, 50 3/8 × 39 1/8″. Kunsthistorisches Museum, Vienna, Austria

Self-Portrait (detail from *The Maids of Honor*). 1656. Oil on canvas. The Prado, Madrid, Spain

Surrender at Breda. 1634–35. Oil on canvas, 10′ 1″ × 12′. The Prado, Madrid, Spain

PAGES 76–79

JAN VERMEER

Dutch. 1632–1675 (*vair*-MAIR)

The Artist in His Studio. About 1666. Oil on canvas, 52 × 44″. Kunsthistorisches Museum, Vienna, Austria

The Kitchen Maid. About 1658–60. Oil on canvas, 17 3/4 × 16 1/8″. Rijksmuseum, Amsterdam, The Netherlands

A Lady Reading a Letter by a Window (detail). About 1658. Gemäldegalerie, Dresden, Germany

A Street in Delft. About 1660. Oil on canvas, 21 1/4 × 17 3/8″. Rijksmuseum, Amsterdam, The Netherlands

Supposed Self-Portrait (detail from *The Procuress*). 1656. Oil on canvas. Gemäldegalerie, Dresden, Germany

A Young Woman with a Water Jug. About 1660. Oil on canvas, 18 × 16″. The Metropolitan Museum of Art, New York, N.Y. Gift of Henry G. Marquand, 1889